How Surnames Began

Surnames are something we all take for granted, only
noticing those that seem to us strange or amusing. But
the names of all of us came into being for very good
reasons, and many of those in common use today – such
as Smith and Brown – have existed virtually unchanged
since the Norman Conquest.

This book explains how we got our surnames, tracing
the origin and meaning of over 800 names. If yours is
not included, take heart, for the author also explains how,
with a little detective work, you can discover its source
for yourself.

Mrs C. M. Matthews was born in New Zealand, but
she now lives in a Dorset village. She has written a
number of books for both adults and children, including
a study of the origins of place names.

40P

How Surnames Began

C.M. Matthews

Illustrated by Peter Dennis

Beaver Books

First published in 1967 by
Lutterworth Press, Luke House,
Farnham Road, Guildford, Surrey

This paperback edition published in 1977 by
The Hamlyn Publishing Group Limited
London · New York · Sydney · Toronto
Astronaut House, Feltham, Middlesex, England

© Copyright Text C. M. Matthews 1967
© Copyright Illustrations The Hamlyn Publishing
Group Limited 1977
ISBN 0 600 34535 1

Printed in England by Hazell Watson & Viney Ltd
Aylesbury, Bucks
Set in Monotype Garamond

To
Mark, Caroline, Lucy and Charles

Acknowledgement

My thanks are due to Mr Philip Mason, the well-known
authority on India and Pakistan, for helping me so kindly
and generously with the section on names from those
countries.

C.M.M.

Contents

1 How Surnames Began

Most people take surnames for granted, seldom pausing to think what they mean. Some, like *Baker* and *Short*, have very obvious meanings; others, such as *Pratt* and *Wray*, do not appear to mean anything at all, and are accepted simply as names. But every surname had a meaning once, and it is well worth trying to find out what it was, because it may tell us something about a very remote ancestor, and furthermore, when all the regular English surnames are pieced together like a great jig-saw puzzle they make a picture of the life and times when they were first spoken.

The system of having a permanent name for each family linking its members together and going on from one generation to another is very practical and convenient. But it was never invented by anyone, never planned or organised or enforced by law. Like many

7

good old customs it simply grew of its own accord because it was needed, and the soil it grew in was conversation. When people wanted to distinguish one man from another with the same Christian name, they would add a word or expression to identify the one they were speaking of, just saying the first thing that came into their heads without any thought on the matter. They might describe his appearance or behaviour and call him the *Longman* or the *Wild*; or give his occupation as the *Fisher* or the *Cook*. Or they might say whose son he was, *Williamson* or *Rogers*, or tell where he was living, perhaps on a *Hill* or in a *Cave*. Such words often repeated could stick to the man for life and even pass on to his children and make a family name for ever. Thus the origin of a surname is seldom an official affair, but a snippet of conversation from the past. It may come from words spoken light-heartedly seven or eight hundred years ago.

These various ways of making an addition to a man's name fall roughly into four groups, which we may call Description (with which all kinds of personal nicknames are included), Occupation, Parentage (or relationship) and Locality. They answer the questions, What is he like? What does he do? Whose son is he? and, Where is he from? It does not matter what order we take them in, for they all developed together and actually our surnames exist in such enormous number and variety that they cannot be fitted into these compartments at all neatly; there are borderline cases between two groups, and odd names that do not seem to belong to any of them. But all the same it is useful to have these four main types in mind, because they help us to arrange this large subject into some sort of order.

When our forefathers first called each other by these second names with no idea of their lasting for ever, they naturally used the most ordinary, easy-going words of daily speech. But English has changed a good deal since that time, which is why so many surnames need explanation today. Some words like those mentioned at the beginning of the chapter became obsolete soon after the Conquest, though not before they had stuck to certain families as lasting labels. *Pratt* meant craftiness and was given to a clever but slippery type; a *Wray* was an out-of-the-way corner where somebody might live. Such words were already old-fashioned by the reign of King John. Their presence in large numbers in the modern world is one of the many proofs of the antiquity of our surnames.

Other words have remained in use in the language but changed their form. *Mylne* is the Anglo-Saxon word for mill; *Reid* or *Read* represents the early medieval pronunciation of the familiar word 'red', a natural nickname for a red-haired man. Others have kept the same form but developed a different meaning, as for instance *Batchelor*, which at the time when it became a surname did not mean an unmarried man but a young knight. So even some of the names that seem quite obvious are not what we think.

But although our language has constantly changed and developed in details, as all living things must, it has also remained basically the same. An amazing number of words and phrases that were used in Anglo-Saxon England are still full of life, and therefore we have among our surnames hundreds of words like *Smith* and *Brown* and *White* that have hardly changed at all in a thousand years.

It is quite easy to imagine how such phrases as Will 'the Fisher', Tom 'of the Little Wood' came to be used in the first place and stuck to people for life. But it is much harder to see how they could pass on to sons and grandsons for whom they were no longer true. For some it was much easier than others. For instance at a very early date many families were known by the places where they lived, and if they continued in the same place it was easy for its name to pass on to the next generation because it continued to tell the truth. This applied both to rich and poor. The lord of the manor was called by the name of the village that he owned so long that even younger sons who settled elsewhere carried the name with them, and in the same way a humbler family who lived by the *Brook* or the *Ford* might always be spoken of in the village as Simon or Robin 'at the ford'. In the two or three centuries after the coming of the Normans the great majority of English people were bound to live and work on the manors where they were born. Nowadays it is unusual for anyone to live in the same house all his life, but then it was the normal thing for working people and families often continued for generations in the same cottage. In such cases the place became identified with them, and when at last a young man leaving the cottage at the ford where he had been born found work in a town far away and his new master asked his name, he would answer naturally, 'Alan Ford'.

With surnames from occupations the process of sticking was often more difficult. The *Miller* was naturally called by his trade, and if one of his sons, as often happened, followed in his footsteps and inherited the mill, he too would have the same surname as a matter of course. But another son might become a shepherd, or a carpenter or a cook, and it would be most unnatural to call him 'Miller'. And yet in time this did happen. We can watch it happening in documents that have survived from the Middle Ages.

In the reign of Edward I (1272–1307) the whole country was taxed to raise money for the king's wars in Wales and Scotland, and the names of all those who paid their tax, many thousands of them, written on sheets of parchment, according to the villages where they lived, are preserved in the Public Record Office in London. They are known as Subsidy Rolls and are the best evidence we can have of the state of ordinary people's names at this time. A century later when Richard II was king, as a boy, another great tax known as the Poll Tax was laid on the people and their names written down again. Not so many of these lists have been preserved, but enough to tell us a great deal.

In Edward I's Subsidy names like Thomas the Miller and Hugh the Baker are probably still telling the truth, but in the Poll Tax both surnames and occupations are given and they are very often contradictory. We see 'John Carter, draper; Walter Cook, sheep driver; Robert Barber, cook', and many more of this sort, proving that in these families the name has become permanent. These lists also include names like 'Simon Shepherd, shepherd', but the very fact that it was necessary to write like that shows that such words used as second names were no longer thought of as giving information. In fact, fixed surnames are established. It was anger at having to pay this tax that caused the Peasants' Revolt led by Wat Tyler, but there is no reason to believe that Wat made tiles himself, though perhaps his grandfather had done so.

You would think it would be just as unlikely for neighbours to call a man Roger *Johnson* when his father's name was not John as to call a man Fisher when he was really a baker, but this kind of name, derived from Christian names of parents, was established extremely early in England. In Wales it was much later before they settled down, and if your name is *Davies* (the son of Davie, a great Welsh favourite) or *Jones* (the son of John with a Welsh pronunciation) the original John or David may have lived in Wales or moved into England in the time of the Tudors or even later. In Denmark and Sweden, where most of the surnames are of this kind, they were still sometimes changing when one generation succeeded another, within living memory. The son of Hans Larsen might be called Peter Hansen and his son Anders Petersen and so on. This is how it was in England in the reign of William the Conqueror, but even at that time the same name was often passed on to a grandson. Very many of our surnames of this type can be proved to have come from the time of the Norman kings.

One might think that personal nicknames, whether simple descriptions like *Strong* or *Little*, or more fanciful ones like *Lilleywhite* or *Smallbones*, would be the very last to become permanently fixed to a family because they were so clearly invented for just one person. But in fact they are among the very oldest of our surnames. Long before the coming of the Normans the Anglo-Saxons used such names to distinguish one man from another; so did the Danes and the Normans, and when all these people merged together in England the tendency to make nicknames was very strong. Some of these early nicknames are well known to us, such as that of Edmund *Ironside*, so called because he was a valiant fighter, and Hereward the *Wake*, who could never be caught sleeping or taken by surprise. We can see many of them in the Anglo-Saxon Chronicle and Domesday Book, and the remarkable thing is that they are nearly all still with us as modern surnames. It does not follow that families with these names are descended from the very people mentioned in these ancient documents. At that date very few of them were passing on to another generation. But they were the kind of names that people used at the time of the Conquest, and very soon afterwards they were sticking fast.

These early nicknames were always more likely to become permanent when the people to whom they were given were outstanding in some way. A man would not be called '*Armstrong*' by his neighbours unless he was a great hefty fellow who could lift huge stones or tree trunks that others could not stir. He would be long remembered in his village, and this would account for the fact that not only his sons but grandsons and their children too would be thought of as being of his family – the Armstrongs. To some extent this kind of thing must have influenced all types of names. And I believe that in most families the particular ancestor whose name stuck was the one who was most talked of and longest remembered, so that his name conferred a distinction even on his grandchildren. When a name has survived two or three generations it was probably fixed for ever, and once the general principle was established the last nameless families came into line automatically.

Taking all the evidence together we can say positively that surnames were settled permanently in England by 1400, but that most of them are very much older than that. Since that date the only new names added to the mixture are those brought into England from other countries, the chief of them being from Wales, Scotland and Ireland. However, the vast majority of the population still have the original English surnames that sprang to life spontaneously in the early Middle Ages, at a time which may conveniently be called 'the surname period'. They come to us straight from the days when Norman castles were being built, when knights were going on Crusades, while humble men were ploughing with oxen, a time when there were still wolves and wild boar in the woods, as well as outlaws. Our surnames are a direct echo of that time, and if we study them we can find out details about it which we might not learn in any other way.

A plan on page 104 shows how 'the surname period' fits into our history.

2 *Village Craftsmen*

Many of our best known surnames come from skilled craftsmen who lived in the time when Norman kings ruled England. In those days there were few towns of any size, and almost everyone lived in small villages, each with its manor house, and its little church, its cluster of cottages and one or two outlying farms. Such villages were almost entirely self-supporting. The inhabitants grew their own food, and made nearly everything they needed, and the principal craftsmen who made the most important things were spoken of so regularly by their occupations that in time these trade names stuck to them and their families and have been attached to them ever since.

Most important of all was the *Smith*, or blacksmith as we would say now. We must not think of him only as shoeing horses, as the last of the blacksmiths still do, for that was only a small part of his work. The smith of ancient times made everything that could be forged out of iron, and that meant tools for all the other trades, as well as weapons for hunting and war. On his anvil, watched by the admiring village children, he hammered blades for swords or knives or spades, cooking pans, bits for horses' bridles, nails, arrow tips, spearheads, helmets, and innumerable other things. A really good smith could fashion chain-mail armour, and repair it when the links were broken. It is no wonder that every village in England had a smith, and every castle too, and that it is the best known and used of all English names.

Another important person in village life was the *Miller*. The corn must be ground, and every good-sized village had either a water mill with its wheel turned by a river or stream, or a windmill on a hill, but several small places might have to share one. The man who kept the mill and lived in it might be spoken of as Dick the *Miller* or Dick of the *Mill*, and the two surnames mean just the same. Or the older forms of the same words might be used, *Mylne* and *Milner*, or *Mulliner*, so that altogether this one word has branched into many modern surnames. This is in great contrast to Smith which has hardly any variations except that some families use the old spelling *Smythe*.

When the corn had been ground the bread could be baked, and the descendants of the *Bakers* are nearly as numerous as the Millers. You might think that in those early times country people would have made their own bread. As far as mixing and kneading went they did make it, but they had no means of baking it in their homes. In the days when such surnames were first being used, cooking was done over an open fire burning on the floor with an iron pot hanging from a tripod for boiling liquids and with pointed spits for roasting. An oven was a separate building shared by the whole village. Often it belonged to the manor-house or castle and the people who lived on that estate had to carry their loaves there to be baked. So the baker who looked after the oven or bakehouse, stoked up the fire to the right heat and saw to the cooking of everyone's bread was well known to all the neighbourhood.

A craft that has made one of our most familiar surnames – one even higher in number than Miller or Baker – is that of the *Taylor*. (As often happens the surname preserves an older spelling than the ordinary word). Again we must go right back to Norman times to find out what made this name so widespread. It was not the making of fine clothes for rich people, for although the rich were very important they were only a small part of the population and we should not have so many Taylors today if their ancestors had not supplied something essential for everyone. The explanation is that at that far-off time they made all kinds of clothing including footwear. When we come to think of it we have practically no surnames from shoemaking. In Germany a great many people are called *Schumacher* (shoemaker) or *Schumann* (shoeman), but German surnames come from a much later date than ours, when shoemaking had become a separate business. In the days when surnames were sticking to families in England the tailor was the skilled man who cut out shoes and leggings and long hose (we would say 'tights' now, but his did not fit so well as ours) as well as tunics and cloaks and hoods. He must often have been the only man in the village to own a pair of shears

17

or scissors. It is likely that the women did most of the stitching, and the wife of an important man would add a band of embroidery round the neck and hem of his tunic.

Leather was very plentiful in those days, far more so than now; for animals were constantly being killed for food, while now most of our meat comes from overseas without the skins. It was prepared for use by the *Tanner*, or *Barker* as he was often called because he used the bark of oak trees in the process. Shoes did not have hard soles and heels to make them last a long time as ours do now, but were made of soft leather that seemed to fit almost like a sock, judging by the pictures and carvings of the period. They must have worn out very quickly, and replacing them must have kept the tailor busy, whereas a jerkin or tunic of strong homespun cloth would last for years.

Although leather was used for many garments, woven cloth both of wool and linen was important too from very early times. First the threads must be spun. But the art of spinning has left hardly any surnames because it was always women's work, so much so that the word 'spinster' came to mean an unmarried woman. In the old records we often see women with surnames from their own occupations, such as Isobella Whelespinner (in the Yorkshire Poll Tax), but such names seldom lasted, for if Isobella married it would be her husband's name that would pass on to the children.

The weaving was done by hand on a wooden loom. In the fourteenth century England became famous for its woollen cloth and has remained so ever since. But long before that time every neighbourhood had its own expert, producing cloth and blankets for local use. *Weaver* is not a very common name, but the much older forms of the word, *Webb* and *Webster*, are very numerous. Like *Milne* and *Milner* they echo forms of speech and pronunciation that were in use in England at the time of the Norman Conquest.

When the cloth was woven it was stiff and rough and dirty, and needed a thorough cleansing and softening before it was ready for use. This was done by another expert who trampled on it with his feet under running water, and was called the *Walker*. We can tell how important this work was in the preparation of cloth by the great number of people with this name which they certainly did not get merely by walking about. Methods of finishing cloth and words used for the man who did it varied from one part of England to another, and in some places he was called a *Tucker* or a *Fuller*, but the Walker who did it in the old style with his feet has made the most surnames.

A very important craftsman with a fine old English name which has long fallen out of use as an ordinary word was the *Wright*. It meant simply a builder, and because it belongs chiefly to the Anglo-Saxon period when most buildings were made of timber it came to imply principally a master-builder in wood. The Normans were great builders of castles and churches for which they mostly used stone, and in time their French words, *Mason* (a stone worker) and *Carpenter* (wood worker) ousted the good old English word 'wright', but not before it had become fixed permanently to innumerable families who carry it still.

Other people who helped with the building of houses were the *Thatcher* and the *Tyler* and the *Slater*, who were concerned with roofs of different materials; but none was as important as the Wright.

Another craftsman whose work has made a well-known surname is the *Cooper* who made barrels, tubs and buckets out of wood, with iron bands to hold it in place. This may not seem a very essential service to us now, but we get our water out of taps, while milk and many other drinks can be had in bottles. In the days when water had to be fetched from a stream or well and ale brewed in great quantity to keep for future use, large containers for liquid were very necessary and hard to make. There would not be a skilled cooper in every village, but there would be one within reach of most of them. If a woman's bucket leaked so badly that she lost most of her water on the way from the river, she might have to walk many miles to the Cooper who could mend it, or make her a new one. It would be an important matter to her and she would speak about him much by this name.

Smaller containers were made in quite a different way by the *Turners*, who used a lathe to hollow out wooden bowls and dishes, or a potter's wheel to make cups and bowls and jugs of clay. The principle is the same in either case, the turning wheel rounded the object whatever the material used. *Potter* is another regular surname for those who made pots of clay or sometimes of metal, but it is not so numerous as Turner, a man who could make many things on a turning wheel.

While on the subject of liquids we should think of the *Brewer* or *Brewster*. In Old English (the language as it was spoken before the Conquest) these two forms of the same word were masculine and feminine, but gradually this distinction was lost and either word was used for either sex. Ale or beer was the regular drink of all classes everywhere, even among the very poor. The brewing was often done by women, and though it is true that most of our surnames originated with men, there must be some families where the original Brewster was a woman, perhaps a hard-working widow who supported her young family by brewing the best ale in the village.

There are several of these pairs of words in which the ending -ster once indicated a feminine worker. Spinner and spinster, Webb and Webster have been mentioned already. In the first case 'spinster' remained exclusively feminine, but 'Webster' was used at an early date for men as well as women weavers. 'Baker also had its feminine, 'bakester', which gives us the surname *Baxter*, but it should not be supposed that this always started with a woman. Another similar pair is *Tapper* and *Tapster*, for someone who served ale from a cask, often a servant at an inn, but again the difference of the genders had been forgotten by the time these words were becoming permanent surnames.

If we collect together the occupations that have made the most surnames we find that their large numbers are due to the skill of the craftsman and the importance of his work. Of all the names that come from crafts among English people today the ten most numerous are: Smith, Taylor, Miller, Baker (with Baxter), Webb (with Webster), Wright, Turner, Cooper, Walker and Mason in that order. The ancestors of these families provided weapons and tools, clothes, buildings, bread, and the means of storing liquid, in fact, the necessities of life.

It might be asked, 'What about the Ploughman? His task was essential, and why is his name not common?' It exists as *Plowman* but is a rare name. The answer is that to make many surnames a craft had to be highly skilled so that it was outstanding in each community. The *Smith* who forged the ploughshare on his anvil was more important than the ploughboy plodding through the mud. Nearly every man in the village could plough his own strips of land, but there was only one smith.

3 Tradesmen in Towns

In the last chapter we thought about the important craftsmen who were to be found in almost every village in medieval England. But there were also many others who made things that were only slightly less important, and who sold their wares in market towns or in the few big cities. There were, for instance, *Chandlers* who made candles. There were many of these in London in the reign of Edward I, but the name is seldom to be seen in village records of the same date, because country people generally got up and went to bed with the sun, and in winter when they needed a light in the dark mornings and evenings they were well able to make candles for themselves by dipping rushes in tallow wax.

Then there was the *Roper* who made rope, and the *Soper* who made soap, and anyone can guess what the

Spooner made. But it should not be supposed that the *Faulkner* made forks. It comes from the 'falconer' who will be mentioned later. Our surnames are centuries older than the use of forks.

In large towns where there were many people needing many things, craftsmen were able to specialise in making one particular kind of object. We saw that in a village the smith did all the metal work, but in early London records we find *Cutlers* making knives, *Naylors* making nails, *Lockyers* making locks and armourers making *Armour*. In the last case the final 'er' dropped off as being a little awkward to say.

Other craftsmen who specialised in weapons were the *Bowyers* who made bows, the *Stringers*, who strung them, and the *Fletchers* who made arrows. This last word, which comes from the French 'flèche' (an arrow), became confused in sound with the old English Flesher, meaning a butcher. In the south of England the new words of French origin, *Fletcher* and *Butcher*, quite displaced the English *Arrowsmith* and *Flesher*, but in the north the old words held their own much longer and made surnames for a number of families.

When we turn to clothes we find the same kind of specialisation. In early medieval London men could earn a living by making just one item of apparel. The cordwainers (*Cordner*) made fashionable shoes of the best leather imported from Cordova in Spain; *Hodders* made hoods (which were the universal form of headwear); *Butners* made fancy buttons; *Girdlers* made girdles or belts, often decorated with precious stones; *Chaucers* made chaussées or what we should now call tights. This word, made familiar by the poet, is really the French version of the English *Hozier*. But Geoffrey

Chaucer never made hose; nor did his father who was a wine merchant. The time we are speaking of when these names were being formed is well before Chaucer's day. When he was born – in the reign of Edward III – surnames were already long established.

All these are rare names because in the villages where most of our ancestors lived, the tailor made all the clothes that were needed. A rich lord living in a castle or manor house would occasionally visit the city and bring back some fancy buttons or a jewelled girdle or a few pairs of Cordova shoes as presents for his family, but the craftsmen who made such things were far to seek. Of all the specialists in clothing the one that was most widespread, according to the numbers of our surnames, was the *Glover*. Gloves were always worn for the popular sport of falconry. They needed special skill in the making and there was a demand for them everywhere.

Of course a great many tradesmen in medieval cities were concerned with food. There were plenty of Bakers in London, but since they were nearly all crowded together in one street the word did not make a distinctive second name as it did in the country. Therefore in towns more detailed names often arose referring to particular items in which one baker or another excelled; one would be known as *Whit(e)-bread*, another as *Cakebread*, another as *Pye*; all names of bakers from the Subsidy Rolls of Edward I and II for London. The last name does not always refer to the edible pie, as it was sometimes used as a nickname taken from the mischievous magpie, but the baking of meat in a covering of pastry is a very ancient English custom, and the same Rolls also mentioned several

25

'Pyebakers', a surname which would easily be shortened to one of its parts.

You would not perhaps expect so many *Gardiners* in towns as in the country, but several are to be seen in these early London taxation lists. We must think of the London of those days as a tight-packed little city surrounded by walls and towers and so crammed with buildings inside that the thoroughfares were narrow lanes. The only open spaces were markets or church-yards, and nobody could grow anything for themselves. Very few vegetables were eaten compared with the many sorts we have now, though herbs were used to a great extent. But the countryside was near, and outside the city walls, especially on the north side, there were many gardens. The Gardeners would bring their produce into the city every day to sell it in the streets; but if too many people were being called by this name and you wanted to distinguish one of them more exactly it would be easy to refer to some particular thing of which he had a good supply. Thus in these early records we see 'Luke the Garlickmonger', 'Adam the Mustardman' and 'Richard Peasemonger', and though these unwieldy names have been shortened in the course of many centuries they still exist as *Garlick*, *Mustard* and *Pease*. But *Onions*, which sounds as if it had the same origin, comes from a totally different source, the Welsh Christian name Ennion.

The *Cheeseman* sold cheese, and the *Honeyman* honey. As there was no sugar, honey was used for sweetening, but people were not used to eating sweet things as much as we do now, and it is an uncommon name. There is little sign of milk among our surnames, probably because it was usually sold by women, who carried it through the streets in buckets that hung from a yoke across their shoulders, and it was only men's occupations that made lasting surnames.

So far all the tradespeople we have mentioned sold only things that they had made or grown themselves. We must now think of some of the dealers whose work consisted only of buying and selling. There were far fewer of such people than there are now. No one has the surname 'Shopkeeper' or even 'Grocer', for general stores did not exist. But there were merchants who sold a few special things that were hard for people to procure for themselves.

One of the most important of these dealers was the *Spicer*. Since there was little variety in foodstuffs in the Middle Ages, and no refrigeration to keep them fresh, people had to make the best of eating a great deal of salted meat and fish in the winter, with little to vary it but a few dried herbs. Bread and bacon were the principal foods of the poor. Consequently, there was a great demand for spices to make the diet more interesting, and to help to preserve the meat in a more tolerable form. From even before the Norman Conquest English merchants had gone on long adventurous journeys across Europe to places where they could meet other traders who had come from Eastern countries where the spices could be obtained. If your name is Spicer you may think of the ancestor who was first called by it as living in an important town and selling small quanties of the precious pepper, ginger, cloves and nutmeg for a high price to those who could afford it. He probably soon grew rich himself in the process.

The favourite spice was pepper, and some traders specialised in this alone. They were called the Pepperers, but the second 'er' dropped off and the surname gradually became just *Pepper*. And as everyone knew that pepper was hot stuff so this word was sometimes used as a nickname for a fiery-tempered man.

Drapers sold the woollen cloth for which England became famous at an early date, and merchants from other countries came to London to buy it. Cloth of silk material, velvet and brocade from Italy, such as the families of rich barons loved to wear, was sold by the *Mercers*. *Skinners* sold skins or furs of many kinds, which were much used at that time for lining cloaks and hoods, and trimming garments. The stone castles that rich people lived in were so cold and draughty that the only way to keep warm in the winter was to wear long, thick, heavy clothes of the warmest possible stuff.

London was a busy port even in those remote days when Norman kings lived in the Tower, which was still a new building rising impressively high above the surrounding houses of wood and plaster and thatch. The river was thronged with small ships bringing the rich fabrics and spices and wines which were the chief imports into England, and carrying English wool to the Continent. The men who manned these ships were not yet called sailors – that word came into use later than surnames. They were 'shipmen', and the surname *Shipman* is still with us, sometimes shortened to *Shippam*.

The Old English word for a man who bought and sold goods of any kind was 'chapman', of which the first syllable meant 'bargaining'. Cheapside was the place where bargains were made. After the Conquest the French word 'marchand' (merchant) came into fashion, and gradually overcame the old 'chapman' until at last it was only used in the country villages and came to mean no more than a travelling peddler, with a packful of trinkets. But it was long after the surname period. In those days *Chapman* was still the regular word for a trader, and its only difference from the grander sounding *Marchant* was that one was English and the other French.

4 The Manor

We come back now to the country to look again at the kind of village that most of our ancestors were living in at the time when their surnames were settling down.

The principal house in the village was nearly always spoken of as the *Hall*, and thousands of families have this name, while only a few are called *House* which also implies 'the big house' as distinct from cottages. As for the word 'manor', which was hardly used at all in common speech in the Middle Ages, it was a Latin term for a complete estate, held and ruled by one man, and centred round his house. It was only later that people began to talk about 'the manor house'. Those who write about history find 'manor' a very useful expression for a whole community bound together in this way, but it made no surname in England.

'Hall' is the Old English word for the home of the lord or leader of a group of people. In the Anglo-Saxon period it was like a big barn, built of timber, where not only the lord and his family but all his followers ate together, and slept on the rushes on the floor or in curtained recesses round the wall. In the centuries following the Conquest the style of living became gradually more civilised. There would frequently be a second room at the end of the Hall where the lord and his family could retire for privacy, and outside there would be many more separate cottages, barns and byres, for the villagers and the animals, who sometimes shared the same accommodation.

The man who was called Roger or Hugh 'of the Hall' was generally not the lord of the manor himself, who would most likely be known by the proper name of the whole village, and would often be away attending the king or some baron who had given him his lands in return for his loyalty. He might own several manors and live chiefly in one of the others. The man 'at the Hall' was often the tenant or steward who lived there always, looking after the estate for its owner. Or he might be just one of the servants who worked and slept in the hall, and the phrase be spoken to distinguish him from another with the same Christian name who worked out of doors and slept in his own hut.

The real Old English word for the official who was responsible for the management of a village and the maintenance of law and order on behalf of the lord was the 'reeve', and the surname *Reeves* must always come from one of these important men. The Anglo-Saxon form of this word was 'gerefa'. Soon after the Conquest the first syllable dropped off, but a number of people still have a trace of it in the surname *Grieve* or *Greaves*. But gradually the word 'bailiff', of French origin, ousted the English 'reeve' which survives now only in surnames. The new word was at first pronounced without the 'f', and the surnames that come from it are *Bailey* and *Baylis*, in several different spellings.

A big hall that was strongly fortified might be called a castle, but only if it belonged to a Norman of importance. We will come later to life in a castle and think now of the smaller 'manor house' with its village and cultivated land around it such as existed in thousands in Norman England.

Such a village was really like one big farm and most of the villagers worked in one way or another for the lord of the manor. Some of them were actually his serfs, and had no possessions of their own, not even their children, who must also work for him all their lives. Others, called villeins, worked on the lord's land only two or three days in the week and were free at other times to cultivate their own small strips; but they were not free to sell their cottages or leave the village or even marry without their lord's permission.

Because so many people lived in semi-bondage it was a wonderful thing to be free. People were always trying to win their freedom in different ways and the subject was much talked of. That is why there are so many people called *Freeman*, or *Franklin* (the French version of the same thing), or just *Fry* which represents the old pronunciation of 'free'. We would never describe anyone in this way now because we are all free and take it for granted. In most villages there were one or two freemen who had their own land to farm in their own time, and could come and go as they chose. Most of them grew rich like the Franklin in Chaucer's *Canterbury Tales*, who was already a fine gentleman. But even they owed some loyalty to the lord of the manor where they lived, and must help him in doing justice in the manor court, and in times of danger.

Generally the smith, miller and other principal craftsmen mentioned in Chapter Two were free, and so of course was the reeve, who was the most important person in the village in the absence of the lord. Other notabilities who helped to preserve the safety of the village from robbers, enemies or wild beasts were the *Ward* or watchman, and the *Hayward*, whose special job was to guard – not the hay as one might guess – but the enclosed fields. (The first syllable comes from the Old English 'haga' from which the word 'hedge' is also derived.)

A person of very great importance to the lord of the manor, and probably an object of envy and admiration to most of the young people, was the huntsman. Hunting was the chief occupation of all landowners from the king downwards. They felt it their duty to kill wolves and other dangerous animals that might harm the precious crops, and to bring in a supply of fresh meat for their household, but it was also their greatest pleasure to do so. Particularly they loved to hunt deer and wild boar, because both gave them exciting sport, the deer bounding swiftly through the forest being hard to follow, and the boar when brought to bay being a fierce and formidable opponent.

The old word for a huntsman was simply *Hunt*. *Hunter* was a later development with exactly the same meaning. This did not signify the rich land-owner enjoying himself on his horse but the highly skilled man in charge of the hounds running with them through the forest with his bugle horn and long sheath knife at his side, knowing every glade and thicket and the ways of the wild creatures, with all the lords and ladies dependent on him for a good day's sport. It is worth noting that although the Normans kept the pleasure of the chase strictly to themselves, denying the ordinary English people the right to enjoy their own forests, yet they relied so much on Englishmen for knowledge of woods that they even came to use the English word 'hunt' (or hunter) themselves. This old word has completely held its own against the French 'chasseur' and 'veneur'.

Another very popular sport was falconry, and this too had its experts, the men who caught wild hawks and falcons and trained each one to perch on its master's wrist in a docile way and at the word of command to fly into the sky and strike down some other bird, one that was good to eat, returning when called to its master. The man who trained these birds of prey and looked after them with loving skill was the *Hawker* or *Falconer*, which as a surname is more often spelt *Faulkner*.

The *Fowler* who snared birds in nets did so in a more practical way for food. Wild birds provided a large part of the national diet and far more of them were needed for a hungry household than the pleasant art of falconry could provide. England was a very different place in Norman times from the land we see today. Besides the forests there were huge areas of marsh and fenland where wild life abounded, and a skilful fowler spending all day among the reeds and rushes with his net could bring back a great basketful of water birds for the evening meal in the Hall where the lord and his household sat down together to enjoy the food they had grown or caught themselves. The *Fisher* too contributed to the feast. Many fishermen lived on the coast and ventured far out to sea in their little boats. But there were lakes, rivers, streams and ponds all over the country, many of them long since drained, and almost every village had a Fisher who with nets and stakes constructed traps for fish of many sorts, and particularly eels, which everyone enjoyed greatly.

Of course the *Cook*, who roasted all these things, or boiled them in cauldrons over the open fire at one end of the great hall, was a tremendous personality. It is no wonder that this word has made such a frequent surname, sometimes surviving in the older spelling *Coke*. Every large household had a cook; even a group of soldiers, or pilgrims, or outlaws in the forest would appoint one of their members to this task. Everyone would be interested in his work and tend to call him 'Cook'. Even kings valued their cooks highly as they did their huntsmen, and in Domesday Book we can see that William the Conqueror rewarded both with gifts of land, so that Tezelin the Cook and Wulwi the Huntsman became lords of their own manors at an early date.

But to return to our village and the special tasks of its inhabitants. Every manor had to have a cart of some sort, and the *Carter* who looked after it and coaxed the team of oxen to drag heavy loads over muddy tracks was a well-known figure. A farm cart of heavy timber

would last for years, and the man who made it would
be long remembered as the *Cartwright* or *Wainwright*,
while the expert who could mend a broken wheel or
make a new one was known as the *Wheelwright* or
Wheeler.

The care of the domestic animals was another important matter. The general word for a man in charge
of them was 'herd', which has given us the surnames
Hird, *Heard*, and *Hurd*, but more often this word made
part of a more exact description. The cow herd has
become *Coward* (which gives a very wrong impression
of its origin); the bull herd exists as *Bullard*; the calf
herd as *Calvert*; the ewe herd as *Ewart*; and the stud
herd, who looked after the stud horses, as *Studdart*
or *Stoddart*. On an important manor where there were
many horses the man in charge of them was the *Marshall*.
We will think of him again when we look at life in a
castle.

The *Shepherd* needs no explanation. Wool was
England's most important product, after food for its
people. Almost every manor had its flock of sheep and
the name would be more common than it is if there had
not been so many shepherds in some districts that it did
not make sufficient distinction.

Swinnard (or swine herd) is much less common than
we would expect. An odd fact about pigs is the number
of different names they have gone by at different periods.
The Anglo-Saxon word for a wild boar was 'eofor'
(later 'for'), which has left us the name *Forward*. This
sounds much better than a 'pig keeper'. Later 'hog'
came into use, giving us *Hoggard* or *Hogarth*. 'Pig' is
last of all. But in fact the swine were generally turned
out into the woods to root for acorns, watched over

by no one but the children, and though they played a prominent part in the village life they did not make an important occupation for a man.

5 The Church

In our survey of village life we have so far left out one very important person, the parish priest. Long before the Norman Conquest almost every village had a little church standing on the very spot where a much bigger one stands today. Norman landowners generally began the rebuilding process in stone instead of wood, using the newest arts of their time, and the life of every village was centred round the Church and the Hall. Though the priest might be very poor in worldly goods, he was singled out from all the rest by his holy profession. In fact he was such a special person that he was often spoken of simply as 'the person', which is just another form of the same word that developed into 'parson', but he might be called 'priest' or 'vicar' too.

If the clergy in medieval England had been allowed to marry, and had families descended from them in the same way as other people, *Parson* might have been our commonest surname, surpassing even Smith. But Norman archbishops brought in a law new to the English clergy, forbidding them to marry. This was not much liked and some of the clergy did have wives and families, but the majority obeyed the law.

In spite of this the parson was such a familiar figure in every community that his name has come down to us as a surname in several indirect ways. In the Poll Tax, compiled when Richard II was a boy king, we can see the names of villagers as they were then spoken, including some like Adam Parsonservant, Henry Parsoncosyn, Alice Priestsysterservant, and Agnes Vikercister. Some of these need a little study before one recognises what they are.

Such names, which are plentiful in the surname period, give an impression of the parson's house as a very hospitable place. He generally had several servants (they cost little in those days) and relations too who lived with him, and these people might acquire surnames from their connection with him. *Priestman*, meaning the priest's servant, is a name of this type that has survived in full, but many of them were too much of a mouthful to last in their original form. Henry Parsoncosyn's family, for instance, may have been so called for a generation or two, but sooner or later the name would be shortened to either *Parsons* or *Cousins*.

Most occupational names such as Miller or Baker are generally without a final 's', because they began by referring to the man himself and passed in the same form to his sons. But *Parsons* and *Vickers* nearly always have an 's' which shows that they were first used not for the priest but for someone belonging to him and living 'at the vicar's'.

Having thought of the parson, we naturally come next to the clerk, a man trained and educated by the Church, but not actually an ordained priest. These 'lower orders of clergy' as they were called were permitted to marry, and the thousands of families called *Clark* are descended from them.

Of all the surnames that arose from men's ranks or occupations, Clark is the second most numerous, passed only by Smith, and the reason is not hard to find. The Clerk had a special skill which made him outstanding in the surname period; he could read and write. At that time even the barons who owned great castles and ruled over thousands of men could seldom read. The first Norman king of England to be able to do so was Henry I who was nicknamed Beauclerk on that account, because it was such an unusual accomplishment. (The Saxon King Alfred had been able to read two hundred years earlier, but the Normans were not so well educated.) Therefore all the great men in the kingdom employed clerks to write their letters, keep their accounts and look after their affairs, and many of these clerks had great influence on the ruling of the country. Others might be humble assistants to parish priests with very little learning. Every community needed someone who could write. Clark is a good surname to have, for it means that the remote ancestor from whom it comes was the best educated man in the neighbourhood where he lived.

After the parson and the clerk several much grander names connected with the Church come to mind, for instance, *Bishop*, *Abbot*, *Prior* and even *Pope*. When we start to think about the last of these we see at once that it could not be related to the real Pope in any way at all, and can only have been given as a nickname, perhaps to someone who was very pompous and inclined to preach, or for some other light-hearted reason that we can only guess. It is the same with Abbot and Prior. An ordinary parson might occasionally have a family, but those who entered monasteries took a binding vow of celibacy, and though some monks broke their vows the exalted men who ruled over great monastic houses had no descendants. Their titles have made regular surnames only because, like Pope, they were used as nicknames.

There is plenty of evidence for this in medieval records. We can see that real churchmen, especially those of higher rank, nearly always have surnames derived from place names – such as William of Wykeham – whereas names like Bishop and Abbot are found among people of a different sort. As an example there is 'Aelfric Abbat' whose name occurs in a twelfth-century list of the tenants of Battle Abbey, in Sussex. He is only a villein, working on the Abbey land and paying sevenpence a year for a small piece to cultivate for himself. And yet his companions have given him this grand name. It could only be done in fun. The real Abbot is a great personage, as high above him almost as the king.

Among all the many names connected with the Church it is hard to draw the line between fact and fancy. It is quite clear that the highest titles cannot be taken seriously. On the other hand surnames that come from the lower orders of the clergy and their dependants generally do tell the truth. Nearly all Chaucer's company of pilgrims which included several of these minor orders are represented among our surnames – the Summoner, for instance, whose unpopular occupation of summoning people to be fined in the Church courts has provided many families with the surname *Sumner*.

In some monasteries ordinary working men from the neighbourhood were employed as servants. Anyone called *Kitchen* or *Kitchener* must have helped in a monastic kitchen, for it was in monasteries that a separate place was first set apart for cooking and this word used for it. A farm belonging to a monastery was called a *Grange*, and the farmer who lived in it was a *Grainger*. A *Monkman* was certainly one who worked at the *Monkhouse* or monastery, and *Monks* probably means the same, but the simple form *Monk* probably started as a nickname, while to call a shy young man a *Nunn* was a good joke.

One thing is clear. The hard-working Englishmen from whom most of us are descended were great humorists. They often showed little respect for the dignitaries of the Church, whom they thought too rich and worldly. This spirit is reflected in the ballads of Robin Hood, in which Robin tells his men, 'These bishops and these archbishops them shall ye beat and bind', but in Chaucer's poor parson we see the village priest whom the peasants were ready to love and respect because he lived among them like one of themselves.

6 The Great Household

A village was a place where working people might spend all their lives. But there was a different kind of community in medieval England that frequently moved about. This was the household or retinue of a rich lord or baron. He might own several castles in various parts of the country and after spending a few months in one of them would move on to another, taking with him a great following of personal attendants, knights, squires, pages and men at arms, with baggage waggons lumbering behind. It is amazing how much those Norman barons travelled, while the king, with the greatest household of all, moved about more than anyone.

Many of the retainers of a nobleman performed the same tasks as some of the village people whom we have already considered. An earl or baron would have clerks to attend to his business, tailors to clothe his household,

43

smiths to keep his weapons in good repair, and other attendants of the sort that were needed everywhere, but there were some who belong particularly to this kind of establishment. Some of their names have risen to high position in later times, but they all began as regular servants.

There was for instance the *Steward*, who was a kind of general manager responsible for all the supplies. This name exists now chiefly in the Scottish form *Stewart*, which is exactly the same in origin. To be High Steward of Scotland was one of the chief titles of honour in the kingdom, and in 1316 Walter the Steward married the daughter of King Robert the Bruce, and their son was the first of the royal house of Stewart. In Scotland, especially in the Highlands where the people were bound together in loyalty to their clans, surnames developed differently than in England. Many men took the clan surname without necessarily being descended from its chieftain. Thus this name was greatly multiplied in Scotland.

Then there was the *Chamberlain* who looked after the chamber or sleeping room. It was his task to see that the lord's bed was prepared, fresh rushes and sweet herbs strewn on the floor, water brought for him to wash in, to help him dress and undress, to comb out his hair, and in fact combine the duties of a valet and housemaid. In a royal palace such intimate attendance on the king was esteemed a high honour, and so in time it became a distinguished title – the Lord High Chamberlain – but that was a very special case. In lesser households chamberlains continued as ordinary servants, often referred to by the simpler form *Chambers*.

In the household of a rich man the *Marshall* was

44

much more important than in a village. The original meaning of the word is 'horse servant', but among the nobility horses were so important that being in charge of them was a responsible position. As with 'chamberlain', this word became a special title at court, so that the 'earl marshal' became the chief organiser of royal occasions (as he still is). But it did not stop with the premier earldom. In modern times it has gone to the highest rank in the army, and then taken flight and soared into the air. But although this name became so grand in a few establishments and in later times, it also continued during the surname period, in more ordinary communities, simply as the man in charge of the horses.

Another household official was the dispenser, who gave out the stores of food, especially the expensive items like spices. He survives among us today in the surname *Spencer*. The pantry or store room where he presided was called the *Spence*, and anyone who assisted him there might be given that name.

We may picture our baron at dinner in the great hall of one of his castles. He sits at a table on a dais or raised platform with his family and any honoured guests, while the rest of the company are at trestle tables in the main part of the hall. His favourite *Page* stands behind his chair ready to serve him with meat or fish. His *Butler* pours his wine, and his *Napier* brings a clean white napkin. The *Chaplin* says grace and the meal begins, a *Harper* sitting on a low stool near the high table supplying a background of music.

The lower tables are thronged with the great man's *Knights*, waited on by their own *Squires* and *Grooms*, and a good company of *Archers* to garrison the castle or follow their lord to war. Among the crowd we see a

Messenger who has just galloped up with a command from the king and is having his meal before returning. There is also a *Palmer* or *Pilgrim* who claims to have been all the way to the Holy Land and back on foot and has a piece of palm in his pouch to prove it. There is always ready hospitality for interesting strangers, and tales of distant lands are eagerly listened to. The *Porter* is at the door, and down at the lower end of the hall the *Cooks* are still busy with their spits at a great open fire.

There are many dogs in the room crunching the bones and other titbits that may be tossed to them and the *Hunt* (whom we would call the huntsman, and whose special pride they are) is at one of the lower tables deep in talk with the *Parker* about the plans for the next day's sport. The Parker is the man in charge of the park or tract of wild country near the castle which the baron has enclosed for his own hunting, forbidding the local inhabitants to kill any of its wild life. The word 'park' suggests a very civilised sort of place now, but in the surname period it was completely wild. The great areas set apart for the king's hunting were called 'forests', and the men who patrolled them were *Foresters*.

This scene in the great hall belongs to another age from our own, and yet all these people who were once part of it are with us in name. Not only do they still exist, but in large numbers, and this fact shows how many households of this type there were and how regularly these words were used. The numbers tell us for instance that by far the most popular form of entertainer was the Harper, who was called just that and not 'minstrel', which is not a surname at all as far as I know. They tell us that 'page' was a much used word, not only in grand establishments like this one, but in other ones where the one faithful attendant was always so spoken of. Otherwise there could not be so many now.

Knights were not only to be found in the retinues of great men. Many of them had been given their own manors where they lived and were known by the names of their own villages; so it was most often landless knights, attending on some more important person, who were spoken of by their rank. A knight at this time was a man trained to fight on horseback. He must own a horse and weapons and armour and be ready to follow his feudal lord to war when called on. His squire who acted as his servant was of the same rank but not yet qualified as a knight himself.

Of course England was full of *Archers*; every able-bodied man knew how to shoot with the bow, and the surname *Bowman* is just another echo of the same universal skill. I do not think any man would have earned either of these names if he had not been greatly renowned for his skill with the bow. It is rather like speaking of someone today as a 'runner'. We should not do this unless the person in question had distinguished himself in athletics.

There is no Soldier among our surnames, for they are older than the use of this word in England. Knight and Archer are the nearest we shall come to it. But there is one more word for a fighting man that we should notice. In the Baron's hall the biggest and brawniest among the Knights was very likely spoken of as the *Champion* (or it might be pronounced *Campion*). In those days legal disputes were often settled by a fight with sword and shield between the two parties concerned; 'trial by combat' it was called. But unless a rich man happened to be young and strong he very often sent one of his knights to represent him. Bishops and Abbots who were often involved in legal cases, because they were great landowners, used regularly to employ professional champions. This form of the word is French, and was used chiefly among Normans. The Old English word for an oustanding fighter, a winner in many contests, was *Kemp* or *Camp*.

It must not be supposed that everyone in the nobleman's household was surnamed by his office or work as has been done in this chapter. Some had nicknames some were called by their father's first name, some by the places they had come from, for in every group a great variety developed automatically, which is why we have so many different names today.

7 Human Appearance

As far back as our records go people were calling each other by nicknames. These might be added to their proper names for futher identification or just for fun. Many have remained with us as surnames, and of these the simplest and shortest are also the oldest.

When we want to describe a person quickly to distinguish him from someone else, we are likely to say that he is young or old, dark or fair, tall or short. But when we consider the first of these comparisons in the light of surnames we discover that there are about a hundred families called *Young* for every one called *Old*. You can see this in any large directory. This gives us a clear indication, which is also shown by other evidence, that the kind of nicknames that lasted best were generally acquired early in life. Most of the

Youngs grew old, and yet the name often stayed with them for life and passed on to their children, who also kept it and passed it on again. But a nickname given to a man when he was already old did not have the same staying power. Therefore, though some of our surnames do describe old men, far more belonged first to young men or boys.

The question of colouring, the second comparison, has given rise to more nicknames than any other. The Anglo-Saxons were on the whole a fair-haired race, but by the time of the Conquest they had intermarried to some extent with the Celtic peoples whom they had driven into the West, and also had a dark strain among them. The contrast must at that time have been much stronger than it is now, when most of us have rather indefinite colouring – neither very dark nor very fair – the result of a long period of mixture. Then, a dark man must have stood out from the rest, while on the other hand there were still many men with the flaxen hair and white skin which had caused St Gregory to remark in Rome that English slave boys looked like angels.

The nickname most frequently given to these truly blond young men was *White*. This may occasionally have been used for a white-headed old man, while *Grey* might apply to middle-age, and so might *Hoar*, which means much the same, but White was constantly used in an admiring way for the young. In Norman French the same sense was expressed by the word 'blond' or 'blund' which became in English *Blunt* or *Blunden*.

But medieval people were full of imagination and did not stop at plain description. Instead of saying a young man was *White* or *Fair* they were just as likely to call him *Snow* or *Frost* or *Swan* or *Lilley*. Or they might call him *Blossom* or *Flower*, or even *Blanchflower* which means of course 'white flower', and was the name of the heroine of a thirteenth-century romantic tale. It must have seemed a good joke to call a man by such a nickname but if this had not happened it would not be a surname now.

On the dark side of the contrast there are just as many names to be found. First the most familiar of all nicknames, *Brown*. We may think of this as an intermediate colour now, but in the early time we are speaking of it was definitely dark. So also was *Dunn*. Then of course there is *Black* about which there can be no mistake, and which has come down to us in another spelling too as *Blake*.

Just as a fair man might be called *Snow*, so a dark one could be compared with coal. This was charcoal, or charred wood, which was much used for cooking in early times and was as black as could possibly be. Long before the Conquest this word had been used both as a nickname and a formal personal name by the Anglo-Saxons and the Danes, and it may often be seen in Domesday Book as Cola, or later as *Cole*. Or a dark man might be called a *Raven* or a *Crow*, or the same thing in French, *Corbin* or *Corbett*.

Much the most noticeable colour for hair was naturally red, which might seem to be missing among surnames, but it is with us in the old pronunciation of the early Middle Ages, as *Reed*, *Reid* and *Reade*, while the Old French version 'rous' has given us *Rowse* and *Russell*. And of course country people did not fail to call a red-headed man *Fox*, one of the commonest of animal names.

Gold and *Bright* probably referred to hair as well. Both these names were much used as men's names by the Anglo-Saxons, who seem to have had a great eye for personal beauty. *Gould* is just another form of Gold.

The only other colour name that exists in large numbers is *Green*, but this has a very different sort of origin which we will come to later. *Scarlett* and *Bluett* (blue) both occur in small numbers and must refer to some very gay cloak or hood that a proud owner wore frequently. Except for Green all the colour names that are at all common describe human hair and complexion.

And indeed hair seems to have been very much noticed. It is generally referred to as 'locks' and beside the simple colour names we have *Whitelock*, *Blakelock*, *Lovelock* (referring to a curl on the forehead), as well as *Whitehead* and *Blackett* (or black head). Then again there is *Ballard* for a bald man and *Pollard* for someone whose hair is cut short.

We come now to the matter of size. In 'the surname period' a tall man was described as *Long* or *Longman*, or even sometimes as *Longfellow*. The Normans used the French word 'grand' and in England this developed a sharper ending and became *Grant*. As this became the nickname of a Scottish chieftain at an early date, it was greatly multiplied in Scotland in the usual way of clan names.

Other ways of describing a tall, thin young man were to call him a *Pine*, or a *Pike*, the long spear used in hunting and war. Or more often still he was likened to a *Crane*, a bird closely related to the *Heron*. Once these long-legged waterside birds were plentiful in

England, but they are now no longer to be found in a wild state. And yet they have left their name with us in three quite different uses in our language. The first is in many place names, such as Cranwell and Cranborne where once they abounded, the second in the surname *Crane*, and the third is the modern word for the great, long-necked machines that tower over our docks and building sites, just as the original cranes once stood in our pools and marshes.

Another name for a thin man was *Bones*, more common in the North of England as *Baines*. A fat man was generally *Broad* or *Bradman* or *Large*. There were also more picturesque terms like *Puddifat* which comes from 'pudding vat', the big round vessel used for boiling puddings. Roger Podyfat was a rich merchant in London in the reign of Edward I. A cripple might be called *Crookshanks* ('shanks' being the old word for legs), or the same name might be shortened to *Crooke*. Medieval people were not very polite about each other's appearance.

A *Small* man could be called just that (sometimes in the form of *Smale*) or perhaps *Short* or *Little*, or even *Littler*. Among French speakers he would be *Pettitt* or *Bassett*, both very old Norman nicknames. He could also be called *Wren* (our smallest bird), or *Spratt* (a tiny fish), or even *Peppercorn* or *Nutt*.

But there is a possible catch in names of this sort. Everyone knows that Robin Hood's friend was called Little John because he was so big, and as these popular heroes belong to the very time when surnames were being fixed, we know that the jokes that they liked represent the same kind of humour that went into the making of surnames. Therefore anyone with one of these 'small' names may reasonably suppose that the ancestor who first had it was a very big man. It is at least a chance.

But in spite of occasional jokes of this sort, most of our descriptive names began as truth, and in the case of these 'small' ones it should be remembered that many were given to boys before they were fully grown. We all know cases where childish nicknames have stuck to people long after they are grown up. *Twigg* and *Sprigg* and *Budd* are certainly in this class, implying young shoots of the tree that have yet to grow.

One thing that medieval people were quick to notice was the way in which people moved. As the ordinary working man had no other means of getting about, many walked great distances and ran too when there were messages to be carried. It would be well known who was the fastest runner in the village, and he would soon earn the name of *Swift* or *Arrow* or the *Hare*. *Ambler* and *Trotter* or *Trotman* had each his special pace. Gilbert *Proudfoot* who was a sheriff of London in the Norman period, must have walked in a very stately manner, *Steptoe* perhaps in a mincing style.

It will have been noticed that almost every descriptive nickname can be expressed in several different ways. The same thoughts were spoken in French or English and though the English word has nearly always made by far the more numerous surnames, the Norman ones add variety. Every idea could be expressed by a comparison with some living creature, or plant, or object, so that there were a dozen ways of saying a man was fair or young. It is this that makes the names so varied and entertaining. It tells us the sort of things that those remote ancestors of ours noticed and talked about.

8 Human Behaviour

As we have seen, many nicknames referred to men's appearance but there were also a great many commenting on their character and behaviour, and particularly on their courage and loyalty in battle. Young people have always liked to find new words to express admiration for each other's exploits, and so although most of our language has remained much the same for centuries, words of praise seem to have changed their meaning with the passage of time more than others. Thus many expressions once used as compliments have different meanings today.

Sharpe, *Keen* and *Smart* were all words of praise for a fierce fighter. *Stark* and *Sterne* both meant inflexible and unyielding. Another good word for a warrior was *Hard* which survives chiefly as *Hardy* (from the French form), and *Harding* (the English). *Moodey* (or *Mudie*) has changed more than most, for it meant 'of noble and courageous mind' (*Muddiman* was a high compliment). *Snell*, gone now from common speech, meant 'fearless and dashing'. *Bold*, *Doughty* and *True* (or *Trueman*) have changed little, but 'brave', the word we would use for nearly all of these now, had not yet come into the language in the surname period.

To contrast against all these, there really are no surnames meaning 'cowardly'. *Coward*, as explained in Chapter Four, has a very different meaning. It seems that on this important point of character any adverse criticism was unbearable, and if anyone was given a nickname like Milksop or Drawback, both found in thirteenth-century London, his descendants would manage to get rid of it somehow. Anyone who has suffered at school from a nickname that he did not like knows how hard it is to shake off, but with a surname that passed on from one generation to another, an opportunity would come sooner or later. One of the English Earls at the time of the Conquest was known as Ralf the Timid, but this did not make a lasting surname, while the 'brave' names like Sharpe and Harding have thousands of modern representatives.

Another well-known early nickname of an un-complementary sort is that of Ethelred the Unready who could do nothing right and failed in his duty of fighting the Danes. This never became a permanent surname for anyone because it was too disgraceful, but its opposite did as *Ready* and *Reddie*; and the nickname of Ethelred's valiant son, Edmund *Ironside* was used again for other brave men and is with us still. In fact it is true to say that though some unkind surnames survive, the ones that people disliked the most have disappeared.

A very cheerful group of names consists of *Gay*, *Blythe* (which has also become *Bligh*), and *Jolly*, which last comes from the French 'joli' but did not originally mean 'pretty' as it does now in France. Another pleasant pair are *Merry* and *Merriman*. The last was the name almost always used in the old ballads for Robin Hood's men, and it may be that is signified an outlaw at the time when it became a surname. *Merryweather* and *Fairweather* are names that can be found in early records of sea-coast villages, where the weather meant much to sea-faring people and such a description implied a good-tempered man.

The Normans were very fond of using nicknames, and when they invaded England in 1066 many of them already had surnames that had arisen in this way. There was for instance Walter *Giffard* who had a fat face ('giffre' means 'jowl' or 'fat cheeks'), and there was William *Mallett* who took his name from the hammer-like club that he swung in battle, and Humphrey Vis de Lou (or Wolf Face) whose name gradually became contracted in English to *Vidler* and has now often become confused with *Fiddler*.

The very first man killed at Hastings was William's minstrel Taillefer, which meant in Norman French 'cut-iron', and is to be found today in such forms as *Telfer*, *Telford* and *Tulliver*. This was a particular sort of name that was popular both with Norman and English, consisting of a verb and a noun stuck together indicating the kind of thing the man could do. The name *Talbot* is another with the same sort of origin. The first syllable is 'taille' again; the second is more uncertain, perhaps a 'butt' of wood, the idea being one who could cut through a tree trunk. In any case it was a personal name by the time of the Conquest. Another of the same sort that is recorded only a little later is *Butlin*. This time the 'but' means 'push' (it seems to be the same idea of a tree trunk used as a battering ram), and 'lin' is all that is left of 'villein' (or peasant). Push-the-peasant was probably a mild way of describing the behaviour of some Norman landowner to his unfortunate tenants. The name has much happier associations now.

The English also liked making up nicknames of this kind and many still exist though not one of them is at all common. The most famous of them, of course, is *Shakespeare*, which was probably first used for a quarrelsome fellow who brandished his spear and enjoyed a fight. In 1487 a young man called Hugh Shakespeare who was enrolling in Merton College, Oxford, changed his surname to Saunder, giving as his reason that the name Shakespeare 'was of low repute'. At that time the original meaning of 'troublemaker' – or something like it – must have been still remembered. If Hugh had lived a hundred years later he might have felt differently.

The English surnames of this type are on the whole milder in spirit than the Norman, though they may contain a note of criticism. *Lovejoy* suggests that its owner was rather too pleasure loving, *Scattergood* that he scattered his 'goods' or money too freely, *Spenlow* (originally 'spend love') that he indulged in too much love-making. *Drinkwater* may mean what it says, but it is much more likely to suggest the very opposite with heavy irony. *Dolittle* was clearly lazy. *Wagstaff* is of the same type as Shakespeare. There are many more names of this sort to be found in early records, but all the nastiest, such as Pickbone and Spillblood, have gone.

Some are highly complimentary. What could be a better name than *Makepeace*, while *Turnbull*, which has attained the highest numbers among names of this sort, applauds the courage and strength of a man who can master a bull. Others of this type belong to special occupations; *Benbow* (bend bow) stands for an archer; *Kellogg* (kill hog) for a butcher; *Culpepper* for a spicer; *Rackstraw* (rake straw) for a farmyard worker; *Burnand* (burn hand) for the official who carried out the cruel sentence of branding a convicted person, and *Catchpole* (catch pullet or hen) for the agent of a landowner who carried off a peasant's best hen as payment for his rent or tax.

One subject that has always caused amusement among neighbours was any kind of love-making or sentimentality, and this mocking note had left us many surnames, such as *Sweeting*, *Sweetman*, *Dearlove*, *Dearman* and *Darling*. All of these were used either as Christian names or nicknames before the Conquest; Aylmar Darling was an English Earl in the reign of King Canute. Both *Sweet* and *Love* were favourite girls' names at this time, and young men did sometimes inherit their mother's Christian names as surnames, as we will see later; but even if they started with girls they had to be borne by about twenty generations of men to reach our time. In general such names were bestowed in the surname period in a spirit of fun. *Fullalove* and *Well-beloved* are certainly nothing but nicknames. That the joke was taken in good part and not much objected to is shown by the large numbers of surnames of this type still current today. So long as they were not called 'cowardly' or 'timid', men seemed able to put up with almost any name.

9 Birds and Beasts

It must have been noticed in the last two chapters that although our medieval forebears often described each other in simple, straightforward words, they were also very much inclined to compare people to birds, animals, plants and objects, and indeed everything they saw and knew. Already we have mentioned a number of living creatures used as types of tall, short, fair and dark people, but many more were used to make nicknames expressing other qualities.

If we collect some of these together we see how well those remote ancestors of ours knew and understood the wild life of the woods and hills around them. They lived much nearer to nature than we do now; the forests and marshes of their England were untamed, and teemed with wild birds and animals. Then again they had fewer distractions than we have – no ready-made entertainment, few books, little in the way of transport. They had to find their own pleasures by looking about them, and they were far more observant than most of us are today.

At that time many popular old tales were current in England about birds and animals, tales in which each creature has its special character. The fox was cunning, the owl wise, the goose foolish and so on. But though our forefathers knew these traditional characteristics well, they also noticed the true habits of the living creatures, or they would never have used so many of their names so freely.

Best of all they knew and loved the birds, looking on them as friends and companions. This is shown in the way people liked to give human names to the most familiar birds, calling them Tom Tit, Jenny Wren, Mag Pie, and Jack Daw. Two little birds were called Robin and Martin so regularly that now we think of these as the names of their species. But they were boys' names first. In reverse bird names were often given to men. Some of these have been already mentioned in the last two chapters. Others with obvious meanings are *Nightingale*, for a very good singer; *Jay*, a flamboyant fellow with bright clothes and a loud voice; *Sparrow*, a lively and quarrelsome little person; *Coot*, a bald man; *Partridge*, a plump one.

Finch is well-known as a surname, and there are many kinds of finches. In fact few people nowadays would know what the name implied. But all the finches are brightly coloured, merry little birds, particularly gold-finches, which were often kept as pets, and their proverbial meaning is 'gaiety'. An old name for the chaffinch was *Spink* or *Pink*, because this is exactly the sound of one of his frequent notes, and this too made a name for a bright, happy person.

Many other bird names exist that we might not recognise. Some have old forms or spelling, while others are words that have become obsolete. A Lark used to be called *Laverock* or *Laverick*, and the Thrush generally *Throssel*. The old word for a woodpecker was *Speight*, which made a good nickname for a carpenter. The hedge sparrow, a quiet little grey-brown bird that should not be confused with a house sparrow, was a *Dunnock*, and a redbreast (when not called Robin) a *Ruddock*. A tit was often a 'tit-mouse' and the surname *Titmus*, though it is not common, is very well known today. This name must I think have been given, like *Wren*, to a very small man, but whereas a wren is a small *shy* bird, a tit is a small *bold* one.

Anyone can find amusement in looking out for more of these bird names. I have found over fifty different species in the London Telephone Directory alone, and though some require special knowledge for recognition, others are quite obvious. The numerous water birds should not be forgotten. Nearly all are there, including *Teale* and *Mallard* and the *Shoveller* whose name describes his mode of eating. This surname, often contracted to *Showler*, must have been given to someone who ate his dinner in this vigorous style.

Of all the birds the one that has made most surnames is the *Hawk*, and this reflects not only the love of falconry in our period but also admiration of the fierce wild, courageous creature with its magnificent powers of flight. Many kinds of hawk may be found in the directory, including the *Sparrowhawk*, which has survived in full length from before the Conquest when a bishop of London in 1050 was so called. A *Haggard* was a hawk that had been trained but gone back to the wild.

But even more common than *Hawke* is the general term for a male bird, 'cock'. From our very earliest history this was a favourite nickname for a lively, domineering young fellow, and by the time surnames were sticking fast in the twelfth and thirteenth centuries it was so widely used that it was often tacked on to the end of a Christian name, making forms like Will-cock, Sim-cock, and Ad-cock (Ad being in this case short for Adam). Very often as it turned into a surname in passing from the original Wilcock to his son it acquired a final 's', becoming *Wilcocks* or *Wilcox*. In this last spelling, as in the simpler form *Cox*, the 'cocky' bird is lost to sight.

When we begin to look for 'animal' surnames there are almost as many. The *Fox* has been mentioned already. He also had another name, *Todd*, now nearly forgotten. A *Brock* was a badger, and the old word for the polecat, a fierce wild creature with flashing eyes and sharp claws, was the *Fitch* or *Fitchett*.

Anyone called 'the *Bull*' was tremendously strong, while 'the *Hart*' and the '*Buck*' implied handsome, active young men, for in the surname period everyone thought a fully-grown stag in the forest a glorious sight. The *Wolf* stood for ferocity, and had been used in naming men from the earliest recorded times.

The most exciting animal to hunt in Norman England was the wild boar because it was so fierce and dangerous. Because its courage was admired, its name, like 'Wolf' was thought fit for a hero. It has sometimes survived in full as *Wildbore*, more often shortened to

Wilber, but the special word most generally used for it was *Hogg*, which meant the fullgrown young male animal. Since those days this word has come down in the world sadly, and is now used chiefly in ordinary speech to denote greed or bad behaviour (we speak for instance of 'road hogs'), but in the surname period it was a compliment.

Many animal and bird names became attached to men because they were connected with their daily work. It would be among fishermen on the coast that a big man would be called *Whale* and a small one *Spratt*. And it would be the fowlers creeping through the woods with their nets, or crouching all day among the rushes, who would know the wild birds so well that a *Quayle* or a *Woodcock* might remind them of one of their friends.

The reason that so many families are called *Lamb* is simply that there were so many Shepherds spending their lives among their flocks that they were bound to make some comparisons from this familiar sight. If a Shepherd's son had curly fair hair, like sheep's wool, it would be very natural to call him a Lamb. When he grew up into a very un-lamblike young man, it would make a good joke, or pass unnoticed, for nicknames given in childhood often stick for life. Other names for young animals are *Bullock* and *Kydd*, while *Bird* originally meant a young bird, the more general term being *Fowl*. *Purcell* meant a little pig, and *Lovell* (a special favourite of the Normans) a young wolf.

It will be noticed that all the names that are at all common come from creatures that were to be found in England, for nicknames sprang from real observation and familiarity. A possible exception among birds is *Peacock*, but although these handsome birds have never been wild in England, they were kept as pets by kings and nobles from Anglo-Saxon times, and were well known. They were regularly used in speech as an example of pride.

The lion was known only by hearsay, to all but a very few. And therefore, though it was occasionally given as a nickname among the nobility (we think of course of Richard Coeur de Lion, and the old Scottish family of *Lyon* from whom the Queen Mother is descended), it was seldom used among the ordinary people whose speech has given us all our regular names. Among the Jews the lion had a special significance, and many of them have this surname, generally in the form of *Lyons*.

But though it is true on the whole that men made nicknames from the creatures that were most familiar to them, there are two strange omissions. No one was ever called by the names of those two friends of man, horse and hound. Were they too near and dear to be spoken of jokingly in this way? There is no easy answer to this question; it is just a curious fact.

10 More Nicknames

Some nicknames sprang from activities that did not belong to the work-a-day world but to plays, pageants and times of festivity. For instance, we have seen that a man might be called a *Bishop* simply as a joke, perhaps because he was fat and ate too much, there being much criticism among poor people of our period of the luxury in which the great church dignitaries lived. But there was also an ancient custom practised in many towns in which a young boy was chosen to play the part of a bishop, dressed in splendid robes and treated with great solemnity for a week. The event would be long remembered and perhaps give him a nickname that would stick for life.

There is no doubt that many surnames come from the acting of religious plays, which were great events

68

in the lives of the villagers and gave opportunity for simple men to use their dramatic talents. At first these plays told only the Bible stories, but later on various moral figures were introduced, personifying virtues and vices, who gave good or bad advice to the leading characters. From these early dramas we get such surnames as *Faith*, *Virtue*, *Verity*, *Wisdom*, *Peace*, *Justice*, and *Mercy* (or *Marcy*). The corresponding vices have not lasted so well, because people did not like being called Gluttony or Sloth and managed to get rid of such names, but *Pride* is still to be found and also Death and the Devil, though both of these dramatic characters are often disguised nowadays by different spellings such as *D'Eath* and *Deville*.

But before these Morality plays developed, the simple Bible stories were enacted in village churches, and the natural favourite was the Christmas play of the nativity. It is from taking part in this that the surname *Virgin* or *Virgo* arose, and perhaps also *Mildmay* or mild maiden. Anyone who acted the part of an *Angel* would have a striking costume complete with wings, and if his own behaviour was not always very angelic his friends would think it all the more humorous to use the name for him. Perhaps *Saint* comes also from this kind of acting.

Of course in the Christmas story there are *Kings* and *Shepherds*, but we can see at once that both these surnames are far more numerous than the others that come from plays, and must have some other regular origin to have produced such large numbers. There is no problem about the Shepherds, for every manor had its flock of sheep, and Shepherd would in any case have been a regular surname. But why are there so many

Kings, twice as many as the Shepherds, ten times as many as the Angels?

The answer is not to be found in reality – as it is with the Shepherds – for when we look in the early records we see plainly that this name has no connection with the real King or his household. It is to be found in the records of hundreds of villages in every part of the land where one of the working men is written down as Jack or Tom 'the kynge'. If we ask how this came about, the answer will be found chiefly in the festival of the spring which took place on the first of May.

In those days winter was a harder time than it is to us. Castles and cottages were cold, and food was scarce. So the first signs of green in the woods were hailed with genuine rejoicing, in the knowledge that good times were coming. 'Sumer is icumen in', sang an unknown poet of the thirteenth century, expressing a joy that everybody felt. Early in the morning on May Day all the young people of every village were out in the woods, gathering greenery and flowers. Then the King of the May was chosen and crowned with a garland of flowers or some more fantastic crown of antlers, and there was dancing and jollity of every kind. Of course there was a May Queen too, and in time the young men dropped out of the ceremony leaving the principal part to the girls. But originally the King was the more important of the two, and the title could stick to a popular young man for life.

This spring festival is much older even than Christianity. Our heathen ancestors in prehistoric times had welcomed the spring in some such way, and traces of their ancient practices lingered long in the May Day games. In many villages the young man chosen for the principal honour was dressed all in leaves typifying the Spirit of the Woods, and then he might be called Jack-in-the-Green, or the Green Man. So May Day is responsible not only for most of our *Kings* but also for a large number of our *Greens*.

Other surnames that may have come from the same source are *Greenwood*, *Greenleaves*, *Garland* and *Greenman*, which has often been twisted into *Grenham*. The surname *May* is obviously close in origin to this group too, though it may also have been used as a nickname for any boy with a pink and white complexion. 'He was as fresshe as is the monthe of May', says Chaucer of the squire in his tale.

The other chief time of rejoicing in which everyone took part was at Christmas, and this too, though a great Christian festival, coincided with the older heathen feast of *Midwinter* or *Yule*. Both these words have made surnames, and so have *Christmas* and *Nowell*. But the commonest surname connected with this important period is just *Winter*. This was often used as a Christian name for boys born during the special twelve days of Christmas or 'the Winter festival', when there were great fires and feasting and fun. We have seen earlier in this chapter that Christian nativity plays were acted at this time, but probably there were also traditional dances and acting in which someone took the part of Winter, or the old year. But though this name may sometimes have become a nickname in this way, there is plenty of evidence that it was also given to children at the font, just as *Noel* may be given still.

We also have the surnames *Summers* or *Sommers*, and these may have at first been names for children born at mid-summer, while Easter is represented by such

names as *Paish* and *Pask* which come from the Old
French word for Easter, 'pasques'. In fact we may say
that in the early Middle Ages the date of a child's birth
was thought very important, and often influenced the
choice of a Christian name for him, or provided a
nickname, and in either case it was liable to pass on to
his son as a surname.

We have seen that the surname King does not signify
any real connection with royalty, and in the same way
we must accept *Earl*, *Baron* and *Lord* and other lofty
titles like those of the Church as all originating in some
sort of play-acting or just a spirit of fun. This can be
plainly seen in medieval records where such names are
to be found most frequently among peasants, outlaws
and vagabonds.

As an example there was 'Adam the Erl', the villein,
or bondman, of a Lancashire parson. At the Assizes of
1246 his master complained that Adam had run away,
and the court ordered that if he were not caught all his
possessions were to be forfeited. But then it was stated
that he had no possessions. Nothing. Let us hope that
he was never captured but found good employment
and freedom far away. He must have been a merry
fellow, or outstanding in some way for his companions
to dub him 'The Earl'.

It might be thought that every possible kind of
nickname had now been mentioned, but as there is no
end to human inventiveness there really is no end to
nicknames. There is for instance the sort of name that
comes from a favourite phrase or word that some man
was always using. That this was a regular source of
nicknames can be seen in Domesday Book where one
of the chief Barons who came to England with William I

is Roger Bigod, whose name came from an oath which must have been often on his lips. Another Norman is set down as Roger Deus-Salvet-Dominas, which in his own language would be 'Dieu-garde-les-dames', and in English 'God-save-the-ladies'. Bigod still exists as *Bygott*. Whether the other Roger had a family who carried on his name is not known, but the surnames *Dugarde* and *Godsave* must both come from something of this sort. A better known name of this kind is *Purdy*, which began as 'Pour Dieu' or 'for God's sake', while a milder expression, used by some kindly person entering a house, was 'God be here', which has survived as *Godber*.

These names undoubtedly come from words and phrases often repeated, and there must be many more in this class, though it is hard to be sure which ones arose in this way. I think for instance that names like *Goodsir*, *Goodfriend*, *Goodbody* and *Fairbrother* often represent someone's manner of speech. A man who lards his speech with polite expressions of this sort can soon have one of them applied to himself. Even more so, in the days when the Norman aristocracy was speaking French an Englishman who tried to add a smattering of French to his conversation might soon be labelled with one of his own expressions such as *Bellamy* (bel ami – fair friend), *Bonser* (bon sieur – good sir), *Bonham* (bon homme – good man), or *Muncer* (monsieur).

These are just a selection of the many different kinds of nicknames which still remain with us today, echoing the light-hearted talk of the Middle Ages.

11 Familiar Christian Names

When you look around at all the modern surnames written over shops and offices, and in school lists and newspapers, you can see at once that an enormous number of them are formed from men's Christian names. They are called 'patronymics', which means that they come from the name of one's father. Many of them are so straightforward that they need no explanation. Anyone can see that the first *Robinson* was the son of Robin. *Robbins* means almost exactly the same thing, but there is this slight difference, that its possibilities are a little wider. It may have been used originally for Robin's brother, or his servant, though in fact the chances are that it was his son, while with Robinson the relationship is quite clear.

Another more definite distinction between these two types is that the addition of '-son' was a regular habit in the North of England and the Lowlands of Scotland, while the form with a final 's' belongs to the South and Midlands and to Wales. This gives an idea of where your family was living in the surname period.

There are far more of these patronymics than you might suppose, and many are not easy to recognise. This is because while they were still being used as first names they were often changed into familiar forms or 'pet names', and passed on to the next generation in this homely guise. To begin with they were shortened. We must remember that most of our surnames arose from informal speech, and it was easier to say 'Will's son' or *Wilson* than the full length *Williamson*. These short forms give us our most numerous patronymics such as *Watts* and *Watson* (from Walter), *Gibbs* and *Gibson* (from Gilbert), *Simms* and *Simpson* (from Simon). As you can see, some letters dropped out and sometimes an extra letter, like the 'p' in Simpson slipped in just because it was easy to say at that point.

But there was much more variety to 'pet names' than just shortening long ones. When William had become Will, his friends and relations might add one of several affectionate or familiar endings, such as '-et' or '-let', '-in' or '-lin', '-kin' or even '-cock' (as we saw on page 65), so that he might end up as *Willett*, *Wilcock*, or *Wilkin* which might be shortened again to *Wilkie*, and produce the surnames *Wilkinson* and *Wilks*. 'Kin' was used especially for young people, and the great number of surnames like *Watkins*, *Simpkins*, *Perkins*, *Tompkins* and so on show how popular it was.

Once you have understood the way in which these many names were formed you can pick out dozens more. But you must think of the sound rather than the spelling. *Hewlet*, *Hewitt* and *Hewetson* all come from Hugh, as also do *Huckin*, *Huggins* and *Huson*. *Nixon* is the son of Nick, and *Dixon* of Dick.

The last example brings us to another way in which these names may be disguised. Englishmen have always had a tendency to vary names in an affectionate sort of way by rhyming them. We like to say Georgie Porgie, and Andy Pandy, and then it has often happened that the second rhymed form is the one used. In this way our remote forefathers turned the grand Norman name Richard into *Hick* and *Dick*, and Roger into *Hodge* and *Dodge*. Many English people have a slight difficulty in pronouncing 'R', and we can see that this is a very old weakness by the great number of surnames created from rhymed versions of names beginning with 'R'. They did not stop at the short forms, but often added a familiar ending to make Hodge into *Hodgkin*, and Dick into *Dicken*. Without some study of medieval 'pet names' you might hardly know that *Hodgkinson* really means 'the son of Roger'.

Thus from one single Christian name we may have twenty or thirty different surnames. When the name Richard first came into England the 'ch' had a hard sound like 'k'. From this form we have *Ricketts*, *Hicks*, *Hickson*, *Dickens*, *Dixon*, *Dickenson*, *Rix* and many others. Some West Country speakers made the 'ck' sound thicker and from them we get *Diggs*, *Higgs*, *Higgins* and *Diggins*. From the softer 'ch' come *Hitchens* and *Hitchcock*; and at a rather later date the more formal-sounding *Richards* (often from Wales) and *Richardson* (from Scotland or the North).

Most of the Christian names just mentioned came into England with the Normans and indeed when we count up the ones that have left the greatest number of surnames (and were therefore the most popular names of the Middle Ages), we find that most of them come directly from William the Conqueror and his family. His father had been Robert, and his grandfather Richard while other near relations were Hugh, Gilbert and Walter. All these names were already common among his followers when he invaded England. His sons were Robert, William and Henry, the last one being born in England after William had made himself king. This name was always pronounced Harry and is responsible for our thousands of families called *Harris* and *Harrison*.

The English as a whole did not take to these names quickly, though some of them who accepted Norman rule because they had little choice began at once to give them to their children. But they spread gradually to the humbler people. If the Norman knight who lived at the Hall was Richard or Roger, the reeve or bailiff who managed the estate for him, and the servants who lived in his household, would soon call their sons after him, and in time even the peasants bringing their babies to the little church to be baptised began to give them the new-fashioned names. But once the grand new name had been spoken correctly over the font by the village priest, the peasants returning to their cottages, soon reduced it in homely speech to Hick or Dick, Hodge or Dodge. Thus these new Norman names were truly adopted by the English, and in time they learnt to say them properly too, so that many of these old rhymed forms exist now only as surnames.

Of all the Norman names, none was more completely taken to their hearts by the English than Robert. As the name of the Conqueror's eldest son it became at

77

once a favourite among the upper classes, and if Robert of Normandy had not quarrelled with his father and lost his inheritance, we would have had at least one King Robert and probably more. But although that unfortunate prince missed the throne and ended his days in prison, his name was already spreading fast from the aristocracy downwards, and when it reached the villagers they seemed to like it better than any other. If a Christian name has branched into many pet forms it is a sure sign of its popularity in all classes. In common speech Robert was almost always turned into Robin, and then rhymed – Rob, Hob, Dob and Nob, but strangely enough not Bob, the one we might use now. Then came Hobkin which easily turned into Hopkin, and the surnames which followed from all these include *Robinson, Robson, Robey, Dobbs, Dobson, Dobie, Hobbs, Hobson, Hopkins,* and many more, as well as the formal *Roberts* and *Robertson.*

But besides all these different versions of this one name there is something else that shows how well English people loved it. They gave it not only to their sons but to all sorts of familiar creatures. The friendliest little bird became Robin, the favourite horse Dobbin or Hobby. (Later 'hobby' came to mean a toy horse, and finally just an amusement. But it is still a short form of Robert.) The magical spirit of the woods, whose older name was Puck, and who might if you were lucky sweep your floor or churn your butter for you while you slept, was called Hob Goblin or in some places Lob, or more politely Robin Goodfellow. If we ask why this particular name was so beloved by the English the answer must be that it belonged to their special hero Robin Hood. Nobody knows exactly when he lived, but it was probably about the year 1200 in the reigns of Richard I and John. At that time the name Robert or Robin was already spreading fast, but in the following century its popularity became even greater, producing these many variations and familiar uses among the country people.

Not all the names that the Normans brought to England nine hundred years ago have remained in favour all this time. Some were used for a short time, and then faded away completely leaving little trace except a number of surnames. There was for instance Reynald, or Ragnald, which has left the surname *Reynolds*, and Haimo which is responsible for our many *Hammonds* and *Hamblings*. Another forgotten name, which was common among the Normans, is *Pagan*, which actually meant a heathen or barbarian. It seems a strange name to give a Christian child, but it may be seen in many early records and the number of people called *Paine* or *Payne* prove that it was once in fashion in this country.

But the really great favourites of the Norman period, those that were most quickly and completely adopted by the English, have never failed and are still among our favourites today.

12 Biblical Characters

We have seen that the surnames that come from Christian names give a true echo of those that were most widely used in the early Middle Ages and that the chief favourites of that time came from the intimate circle of William the Conqueror's own family. These typically Norman names, William, Richard, Robert, Henry, Walter, Roger and Hugh, are all of ancient heathen origin, but about the time of the Conquest the Normans themselves began to use also the names of Saints from the Bible, and these too spread rapidly in England.

At this time the English had already been Christian for about four hundred years, far longer than the Normans, but they had never been in the habit of giving Biblical names to their children, because of their deep feeling of respect for these holy names. However, when the rulers of the land began to use them everyone else followed the new fashion.

The first royal person to have a Biblical name in England was King *Stephen*. He was the son of William the Conqueror's daughter, Adela, and in his father's family the name Stephen had been used before in honour of King Stephen of Hungary who had converted all his country to Christianity about the year 1000. Of course it was the earlier St Stephen of the New Testament, stoned to death for his belief in Jesus, who had made the name honoured in Europe first, but the Hungarian king, who was a modern man to the Normans, gave it a new interest for them. Finally the fact of its being the king's name – incompetent ruler though he was – caused it to spread in England just at the right time to pass on to innumerable families as *Stevens* and *Stevenson*.

The only other king of England with a name from the Bible was John, one of the worst kings we ever had. But in spite of that it soon became a favourite. St John the Apostle, 'the disciple whom Jesus loved', and St John the Baptist were both such important saints that as soon as people were used to the idea of using such sacred names nothing could check their increase. About the year 1200 (when King John had just begun to reign) the commonest name in England was William, but by 1300 it was John. Ever since that date these two names have alternated in public favour with Robert not far behind. A century ago William was in the lead, but now it has slipped back and John is an easy favourite again.

Some of the many surnames derived from John, besides the obvious *Johnson*, *Johns* and *Jones* are *Jennings*,

Jenkins, Jackson, Jacks, and even *Hankin* and *Hancock.*
It came into England as Jehan or Johan and was soon
shortened in common speech to Han, Jan, Jen, and last
of all John. Then familiar diminutive endings were
added in the usual manner, making such names as
Hankin and Jankin. This last one was quickly shortened
again to Jank and then Jack which became the general
favourite. John is a name that has split into an amazing
variety of forms in every part of Europe.

The names of all the Apostles except Judas have
made great numbers of surnames, proving their
popularity in the surname period. Peter was in those
early days more often spoken of as Simon, his earlier
name before Jesus gave him the name of Peter, and this
has resulted in hundreds of families being called *Simms,
Simpson, Simmons* and *Symonds.* (We see here several
examples of the extra letters that insert themselves in
familiar speech, like the 'd' at the end of the last example, which just rounds it off.) Simon Peter's second
name came into England first in a French form something like Pierre or Per, and the names that come from
that are *Perkins, Parkinson, Pears, Pearce* and *Pearson,*
but in time the more learned way of spelling it affected
the pronunciation, and so we have many examples of
Peters too, formed rather later.

Another favourite name from among the Apostles
was Thomas, and this became even more popular after
the whole country was shocked by the murder of
Thomas Becket in Canterbury Cathedral. His shrine
there became a place of pilgrimage and many of those
who rode there, like the jolly company in Chaucer's
tale, must have named their next son after the murdered
archbishop. Consequently we have thousands of

Thompsons (with and without the 'p'), *Tomkins, Tonkins, Tonks, Tomlinsons, Tamlins, Tamblyns* and many more forms, The plain *Thomas* is frequently Welsh where the name also became popular.

Some well-known surnames from apostolic names are *Andrews* (*Anderson* in the North), *Phillips, Phelps, Philpots* (from the pet-name *Philipot*); *James* and *Jameson*; *Matthews, Matheson* and *Mayhew*; and *Bartholomew* which became exceedingly popular in the thirteenth century, branching into many pet-names and giving us *Bartelmy, Bartlett, Batten* and *Bates*.

Of names that belong purely to the Old Testament by far the most numerous in the surname period was Adam, which has given us not only *Adams* and *Adamson* but also *Addison, Addis, Adcock* and *Adkins*, which nearly always became *Atkins* or *Atkinson*. When we look for the reason of this popularity we think again of the religious plays which villagers used to act in their churches or in the market places of their little towns. The story of Adam and Eve was the usual beginning for any series of plays, and these two were the most familiar of all the Old Testament characters.

Noah and the flood also made a popular dramatic theme, and this name was sometimes given to boys in the old form of Noë which eventually produced the surnames *Noyes* and *Noyce*. *Abraham, Isaac* and *Jacob* were used occasionally too and *Daniel* was liked because of the lions' den, but none of these compared in popularity with *Adam*.

Yet another well-known story was that of David and Goliath, and the name of David has long been a favourite in England. But the large numbers of the surnames arising from it are due principally to the patron saint of Wales as we will see in the next chapter. The name of David's wise son Solomon was known and respected, but it came into England in the French form Salamon, and has survived here as the surname *Salmon*.

A great influence on Christian names in the surname period came from the Crusades. In 1097 many Englishmen and Normans made the adventurous journey to the Holy Land to try and help capture it from the Turks under the leadership of William I's son, Robert of Normandy, and again in 1189 the war-like Richard I led a large English contingent on the same mission. When the English knights and their followers returned at last to their homes, the Bible stories had become far more real to them than ever before, their knowledge was greatly widened and their minds full of new ideas. Among the new names that these Crusaders brought into fashion in England was that of the prophet Elias or Elijah. They spoke of it in the Old French form, Elie or Elis, and as *Ellis*, *Elliot* or *Elkin* it became a regular Christian name for a time in England. Some Crusaders who had actually reached the river Jordan in which Jesus was baptised had filled flasks with its precious water and brought them all the way back to their English homes to baptise their children, and sometimes the baby boy was christened with the name *Jordan*, which in due course passed on as a surname, one with a direct link with a Crusader.

One more Biblical figure who has named countless families is Michael the Archangel. The name must have been originally pronounced with a soft 'ch', for it survived chiefly as *Mitchell* and *Mitcheson*. The special day of St Michael and All Angels, known as Michaelmas, coming at the end of the summer, was one of the great church festivals, and this must often have caused boys born about that time to be given this name. But apart from that, the glorious figure of an armed warrior angel with wings spread and sword in hand must have appealed strongly to the minds of simple village people. We must remember that the only stories they knew besides the old superstitious tales of elves and goblins passed down from their forefathers were those told them by the priest in church. Their only pictures were the paintings on the church walls or carvings over its doorways or round the font. If we study the earliest carvings and fragments of frescoes in our parish churches we find that the commonest subjects are the twelve apostles, often in a formal row, their faces long obliterated, Adam and Eve, the nativity scene, and Michael conquering Satan, and these subjects known so well to these imaginative people provided names for their children equal in popularity with those of the kings and barons who ruled over them.

13 Later Saints

We have seen that the people of the Middle Ages loved to give their children the names of saints to be their patrons in heaven, especially those of the Apostles. But there were many other saints and martyrs who lived after the time of the Bible, some told of only by hear-say, some well known, and to many of these later saints great devotion was also given. Some, like St Thomas of Canterbury, were modern men alive in the middle of 'the surname period', others had lived several centuries before in the time when the Roman Empire was in a state of decline, barbarians triumphing every-where and traditions of law, order and learning kept alive here and there only through the efforts of the Christian church.

In the British Isles the torch of Christianity was kept burning all through these Dark Ages, as they are called, in Wales and in Ireland. And in the sixth century when the heathen Angles and Saxons had overrun the rest of what is now England, the Welsh St *David* founded a monastery on the promontory in Pembrokeshire where the smallest town in the country to be called a 'city' still bears his name. The Welsh have long memories and the name of their patron saint has always been their first favourite, often shortened to Davie, with the result that innumerable families who came originally from Wales bear the name of *Davies* or *Davis*.

But names originating from St David are not all Welsh by any means. The Anglo-Saxons had not been long settled in England when they were converted to Christianity, chiefly by the mission of St Augustine, and by the time of the Conquest they and the Normans who overcame them were both deeply religious. This was a time when everyone loved going on a pilgrimage; such a journey was a change from daily life, and the religious object made all the hardships worth while. A pilgrimage to St Davids, whether undertaken by sea, or overland through wild mountains where there might be wolves or robbers at every turn, was the kind of adventure they enjoyed, and became extremely fashionable in the Norman period. As a result, the cathedral in this lonely spot was rebuilt and enriched, and David became a popular name in England too, often to be found in thirteenth-century records. The pet-name formed from it in England was *Daw*, which accounts for all our many *Dawsons*.

In Scotland two early kings were called David, so that the name became popular there too. And it must also be remembered that the Old Testament David is greatly honoured among Jews, and that many of them settling in England in recent years use family names derived from this same source.

St *Patrick* like St David was born in the island of Britain, but a little earlier in time before the Roman Empire had completely broken up. As a boy he was carried off by pirates to Ireland, where many years later he succeeded in spreading the Christian faith. His name had less influence on our surnames than David but it has given us a number of *Pattersons* and *Patons*, chiefly from the North, where Irish monks came in the seventh century, bringing traditions of his teaching.

After Patrick and David we naturally think of St *George*, but strangely enough his name was little known in England during the surname period. Many of the families who have this surname acquired it at a later date in Wales when it had at last come into general use.

St George's life was in every way remote from England. He was a Roman soldier in Asia Minor who was put to death as a Christian about the year 300, but little more is known of him for certain. We cannot really believe now that he killed a dragon, but he must have performed some wonderfully brave act for this story to have been told about him and his fame to have spread all over Eastern Europe as it did.

It was during the Crusades that English and Norman soldiers became attached to George. As they fought at the seige of Antioch in 1089 it seemed to them that St George and St Maurice appeared among them as knights on horseback leading them to victory. *Maurice* was also a Roman soldier, the captain of a legion in Switzerland, who was martyred with all his men because he refused to sacrifice to heathen gods. The Normans admired him greatly, in fact they seem to have thought more about him than St George, for Maurice became a common name in England soon after the Conquest while George was still unknown.

The exact meaning of Maurice was 'moorish' or 'dark like a Moor', and this seems to have made the name even more popular, for it was often used as a nickname for a dark-haired young man, especially for one who came from a foreign place. Although the Moors were enemies to be overcome, they were admired as fierce fighters and this nickname was well liked. It is impossible to say when the surname *Morris*, comes from this nickname and when from the Christian name, but *Morrison* is normally from the latter.

In the Third Crusade the English army, led by Richard I, used the name of St George as a battle cry but it was still a long time – two centuries or more – before it became familiar to the English people as a whole. It never branched out into 'pet-names' such as swell the numbers of surnames from more popular saints. We have only to think of *St Laurence*, for instance, another early Christian martyr, to see the difference. From him we have *Lawrence*, *Lawson*, *Larkin*, *Laurie*, *Lowry* and many other forms, but from George only the one form and that not very numerous.

Of all the saints who lived after the writing of the Bible two stand out as supreme favourites, St Martin and St Nicholas.

Martin was yet another Roman soldier, but he was not called on to suffer martyrdom, for he lived at the time when the Roman emperors themselves had at last become Christian, and official persecutions had ended. His life's work was the conversion of Gaul – which we now call France – and the founding of great monasteries there. Many endearing stories were told of this gentle saint, as for instance how on a bitter day he tore his good cloak in two to give half to a shivering beggar. That night in a dream he learnt that the beggar was Christ himself.

Martin was much loved and honoured all over the British Isles long before the Norman Conquest, and the very first Christian church to be built in England (St Martin's at Canterbury) had been dedicated to him. As soon as English people began the practice of calling their children by the names of saints, Martin was one of their first favourites.

St *Nicholas* was a Bishop in Asia Minor who lived in the fourth century after the life of Christ. Very little is known of him as historic fact, but so many stories were told of his kindness and generosity, especially to children, that he must have been a wonderful person in reality to be remembered in this way. His habit of putting presents in poor people's houses secretly by night (wanting no thanks himself) gave rise in the course of centuries to the modern idea of Santa Claus, aided by the fact that St Nicholas' special day falls near Christmas time. The many examples around us of *Nicholls*, *Nicholson*, *Nixon* and so on, in many varieties of spelling, show how much this saint was loved in early medieval England, even though he lived so far away. One of the many pet-names formed from Nicol, as it was then pronounced, was Colin; hence the large numbers of *Collins*.

In the surname period many boys were called after St *Benedict*, a sixth-century Italian hermit who founded the great monastic order known by his name. Nearly all the early monasteries built in England were under the Benedictine rule, and his name was much in use but always spoken in the simple English form *Bennett*, now a well-known surname. Most of our *Bensons* were originally 'the son of Bennett' and not of Benjamin.

Another Italian name with a well-known English form is Augustine. There were two saints of this name, the one best known to us being the first Archbishop of Canterbury, who brought Christianity to Kent in 579. In England his name was spoken as *Austin*, and the well-known surname shows that it was once much used as a Christian name.

It was St *Gregory* who sent St Augustine to England, and he too was remembered and honoured all over Europe, not especially for this act, but as a wise and far-seeing Pope. His name survives not only the full form but also in *Gregson*, *Griggs* and *Grier*. In Scotland it named the great clan *McGregor*.

There are of course many more surnames from the names of saints, *Vincent* (*Vince* and *Vinson*), *Clement* (*Clemence* and *Climpson*), *Anthony*, *Leonard*, *Jerome*, *Giles* and *Hillary* are just a few. They can all be found in the *Oxford Dictionary of Christian Names*, or any dictionary of Saints, and anyone whose family name is of this sort can easily find out more about its origin and perhaps think for himself what brought it into favour in this country.

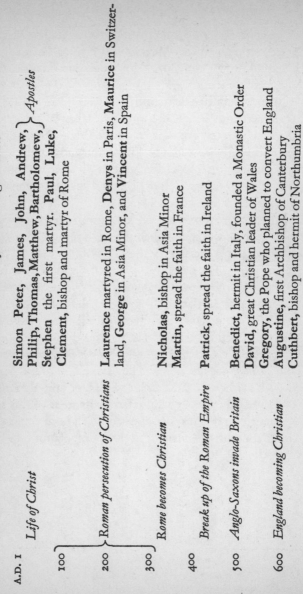

The Spread of Christianity

showing the Saints who have had most influence on English names

A.D. I		
	Life of Christ	Simon Peter, James, John, Andrew, Philip, Thomas, Matthew, Bartholomew, } *Apostles* Stephen the first martyr. Paul, Luke, Clement, bishop and martyr of Rome
100		
200	*Roman persecution of Christians*	Laurence martyred in Rome, Denys in Paris, Maurice in Switzerland, George in Asia Minor, and Vincent in Spain
300		
	Rome becomes Christian	Nicholas, bishop in Asia Minor Martin, spread the faith in France
400	*Break up of the Roman Empire*	Patrick, spread the faith in Ireland
500	*Anglo-Saxons invade Britain*	Benedict, hermit in Italy, founded a Monastic Order David, great Christian leader of Wales Gregory, the Pope who planned to convert England
600	*England becoming Christian*	Augustine, first Archbishop of Canterbury Cuthbert, bishop and hermit of Northumbria

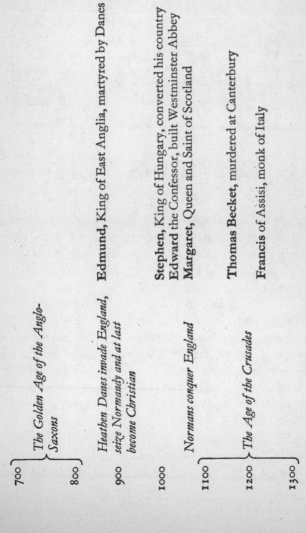

700
800 } *The Golden Age of the Anglo-Saxons*

900 *Heathen Danes invade England, seize Normandy and at last become Christian*

1000

1100 *Normans conquer England*

1200 } *The Age of the Crusades*

1300

Edmund, King of East Anglia, martyred by Danes

Stephen, King of Hungary, converted his country
Edward the Confessor, built Westminster Abbey
Margaret, Queen and Saint of Scotland

Thomas Becket, murdered at Canterbury

Francis of Assisi, monk of Italy

14 Old English Names

It is a strange and surprising fact that nearly all the best known English Christian names came into general use only after the Conquest. We must ask now what the English people were called before that time, and what happened to these older names.

The Anglo-Saxons had very distinctive names of their own, and a very great variety of them for they were always inventing new ones. When they had a new-born son to name they did not think of calling him after his father, or the king, or a saint, but made up a special name for him with a good meaning such as Eg-bert (sword-bright), or God-win (good-friend), or Wulf-ric (wolf-ruler). As long as this system lasted it was rare to have two men in one family or village with the same name, and surnames were seldom necessary, but as soon as the new fashion of calling children after famous men or their own relations became general, a few Christian names became too popular and second names were needed to distinguish people. Thus this change of fashion was an important step in the growth of surnames.

Of the numerous Christian names used by the Anglo-Saxons very few are remembered today. These few are the names of great men who live on in our history because of their achievements: Alfred, the marvellous king who saved England from the Danes, Edward, Edgar and Edmund, descendants of his royal line, and that other Edmund of East Anglia, shot to death with arrows by the Danes. Then there was Oswald, Christian King of Northumbria, also killed by heathen enemies, Cuthbert the gentle monk who loved to live alone among the sea birds and seals, and a few more. But there were literally hundreds of other different names used by these early ancestors of ours that are hardly known by anyone today. In 1066 they were the names of the English people, but two hundred years later they had almost completely vanished.

It was just at this time, when the Anglo-Saxon names were at their lowest ebb, and even the most famous of them almost forgotten, that the king, Henry III, himself of Norman descent, began to re-build Westminster Abbey and re-glorify the shrine of its founder Edward the Confessor. And in his enthusiasm Henry gave the name of this Saxon king to his eldest son, later calling his next son Edmund. Thus these two old names that were rapidly falling into disuse were brought back into fashion again through royal favour. But this happened a little late to cause many English surnames, and many of the families called *Edwards* today are of Welsh descent.

But there was no attempt to revive the great name of Alfred until the very end of the eighteenth century when George III gave it to his youngest son, and like most of the Anglo-Saxon names it was almost completely out of use for about six hundred years. A few of them were revived in the nineteenth century, but many more of the same sort are still unknown.

And yet a great number of these early names are with us still as surnames. They had become fixed forever in this way in the years following the Conquest before they went out of fashion, and their chief interest lies in their great age. If your surname comes from one of the Norman names it could have been fixed soon after the Conquest, or several centuries later; but an Old English one such as *Alfred, Edgar* or *Godwin* could only have come from Saxon people who clung to their old traditions in the days when the battle of Hastings was still a living and sorrowful memory. With these we must include the Danish names that were current in England before the Conquest, which were so like the Old English ones that they are often hard to distinguish from them. Harold, for instance, was a Danish name.

Unfortunately most of these early names are difficult to recognise, either because the original name is unknown to us or because it has been so much knocked about by the passage of time, but they undoubtedly exist in large numbers. Here is a list of a few of them, showing the kind of ways in which they have changed. It will be seen that they are made up of two short words put together, some of them used in many different names. One of the favourite beginnings, Ethel or Athel (both originally Aethel), which had been much used by the Kings of Wessex, usually became simply Al-, El-, or Ayl-. The hard 'c' at the end of 'ric' nearly always became a soft sound as it did in 'Richard'; and sometimes an extra letter crept in, such as the 'd' in *Aldridge*, which, like the 'p' in Thompson, is just a sound that comes easily at that point.

The original names are given in somewhat simplified spelling, followed by their meanings and some of the modern surnames derived from them.

ALDWIN	old friend	*Alden, Auden*
ALFRIC	elf ruler	*Al(d)ridge, Eldridge*
ALFSIG	elf victory	*Elsie, Elsey*
ATHELSTAN	noble stone	*Atherston, Alston*
CUTHBALD	famous bold	*Cobbold*
CUTHBERT	famous bright	*Cuthbert, Cubitt*
CYNEBALD	family bold	*Kemble*
CYNERIC	family ruler	*Kenrick*
CYNEWIG	family warrior	*Kenway*
DEORWIN	dear friend	*Darwin*
EDMUND	rich protector	*Edmonds, Edmunds*
EDRIC	rich ruler	*Edrich*
EDWARD	rich guard	*Edwards*
ETHELBERT	noble bright	*Albert, Allbright*
ETHELGAR	noble warrior	*Algar, Elgar*
ETHELMAR	noble famous	*Aylmer*
ETHELRIC	noble ruler	*Etheridge*
ETHELWIN	noble friend	*Aylwin*
GODRIC	good ruler	*Goodrich, Goodridge*
GODWIN	good friend	*Godwin, Goodwin*
GOLDWIN	golden friend	*Goldwyn*
HEREWARD	army guard	*Harward*

LEOFRIC	loved ruler	*Loveridge, Leveridge*
LEOFSIG	loved victory	*Livesy*
LEOFWIN	loved friend	*Lewin*
OSGOD	divine good	*Osgood*
OSWALD	divine power	*Oswell*
RADWIG	red warrior	*Reddaway*
SAEWULF	sea wolf	*Self*
SIGWALD	victory power	*Sewell*
SIGWARD	victory guard	*Seward*
THURKETTLE*	Thor's cauldron	*Thirkill*
THURSTAN*	Thor's stone	*Thurston*
WIGMUND	warrior protector	*Wyman*
WULFGEAT	wolf hero	*Wolfit*
WULFRIC	wolf ruler	*Wooldridge*
WULFSIG	wolf victory	*Wolsey*

Most of these names now sound to us like surnames and nothing else, but every one of them was a Christian name in Anglo-Saxon England, and there are many, many more of the same sort.

Of course the Saxons did not always call each other by their full-length names, but often used only one part, calling a friend *Good*, or *Winn*, or *Wolf*, and these shortened forms exist as surnames in large numbers. To these the familiar ending '-ing' was often added to make a name for a child or a friend. When a man was called *Brown*, and this was often used as a Christian name (as Bruno is in Italy), as well as a nickname, it could easily turn into *Browning*, meaning 'little Brown' or 'young Brown', just as we might now say 'Brownie'.

All the surnames ending in '-ing' such as *Gooding*, *Whitting*, *Harding*, *Manning* and many more began as

* Danish names.

Old English personal names, reduced to a familiar form. They take us right back to the easy-going, informal speech of the English people as it was in the days before Duke William sailed from Normandy.

15 *Women's Names*

We have been thinking in the last four chapters of the many surnames formed from the Christian names of people's fathers, but there are some – though less well known – that come instead from their mothers. This happened especially in the case of widows. If a boy was brought up by his mother, and she was a lively character well known in her community, the neighbours would be likely to refer to him by her name. Supposing she was Alice or Emma, he would easily become Tom *Allison*, or *Emms*, or *Empson*. He might be called Tom *Widdowson*, but those who talked about him and his mother most were much more likely to use her personal name.

What is more they generally used it in its most familiar form. Pet-names for girls were made in much the same way as for boys, first by shortening and then adding a new ending. Favourite endings for girls' names were -et, -ot, -on and -y. If they later became surnames they might have the further addition of -son or -s, or remain unchanged. The royal name Isabel, for instance, shows us the sort of thing that happened. It became popular early in the thirteenth century after King John had married Isabella of Angoulême, but among ordinary folk it soon became just Ib or Ibbot, or was rhymed to Nib or Bib, so that surnames that come from it include *Ibson*, *Ibbotson*, *Nibbs*, *Niblett*, *Libby* and *Bibby*, as well as *Bell*, which was chiefly used among the French. Mary often became *Marriott* or *Marion*, which have both made surnames, and also Mally and Molly which have given us *Malleson*, *Mollison* and *Moll*.

The two girls' names that were most widely used in the surname period were probably Matilda and Margaret, and it is always of interest to try and find out why a name is popular at a particular time. In the case of Matilda there is no difficulty at all, for this was the name of four Norman Queens. The first Matilda was William the Conqueror's wife; then when his son Henry I married a Scottish princess she took this name as being suitable for a queen. When Henry died – his heart broken by the death of his only son in the White Ship – his daughter Matilda and his nephew Stephen both tried to seize the throne. After a struggle Stephen was successful and, of course, his wife was called – Matilda.

So it is not to be wondered at that there were many Matildas throughout the land, but the name, as was usual with a popular one, was knocked about in common speech. Some used a shortened form of the first part in the form of *Mault* or *Maude*, others made more of the middle syllable which has given us surnames like *Till*, *Tilly*, *Tillett* and *Tilson*. Since those days Matilda has gone out of fashion more completely than any other royal name, but has left at least a dozen different surnames.

The name Margaret also became widely used because of a queen, and one whose life is like a romantic story. She was an English princess of the House of Wessex, a grandchild of Edmund Ironside but born far away in Hungary. When the Danes were attacking England her father had been taken away to safety, as a young child, to the court of the hospitable King Stephen of Hungary. There he grew up and married and had three children, spending nearly all his life in exile. At last when his uncle, Edward the Confessor, was king, he returned to England with his family, but almost immediately died, and soon afterwards the king died too. Margaret's brother Edgar, 'Child Edgar' as they called him, should then have been king, but he was too young, and so Harold, who was no real relation but a good soldier, was chosen instead. Everyone knows that Harold was killed at Hastings in 1066. After the battle, when the victorious William had been crowned in London, Margaret and her brother and sister escaped by sea, with a few loyal friends. High winds drove their small ship northwards until at last they landed on the coast of Scotland. The young King of Scots, Malcolm, received them kindly and soon fell in love with Margaret. At first she would not marry him, but at last agreed if he promised to lead a more Christian life. They had many happy years together and so great was her influence for good over the court and country that she was in time recognised as a saint. It was her daughter Edith who married Henry I, an event that caused great rejoicing in England because it united this Norman king with the old English royal line.

This is why Margaret became popular as a girl's name both in Scotland and England at a very early date, and unlike Matilda has continued so ever since. Like all popular names it branched into many forms, including Meg, Peg, Madge and Margery, which are all reflected in surnames. We have families called *Margetts*, *Margerison*, *Maggs*, *Magson*, *Meggeson*, *Moggs*, *Moxon*, *Pegson*, *Paxon*, and many more, all taking us back to this one name.

Some other surnames that come from girls' Christian names are *Maudling* from Magdalen, *Casson* from Cassandra, *Cecil* from Cecily, *Beatty* and *Beaton* from Beatrice, and there are many more. They cannot always be distinguished from the corresponding boys' names, but *Christie* for instance is probably more often from Christina than from Christopher which was little used in England before 1400, and *Denny* often comes from a feminine form of Dennis. There are none of this class that are very common, but they are an interesting group and account for many rare surnames.

As with those from men's names many of these feminine ones hark back to typical Anglo-Saxon favourites. Edith, name of the last two Queens before the Conquest, exists as *Ede*, *Eady*, *Edis* and other forms, while that of Lady Godiva is echoed in the surnames *Goodeve* and *Goodey*.

Loveday is another Old English girl's name that lasted long enough to make some surnames; and as mentioned before both *Sweet* and *Love*, though used later as teasing

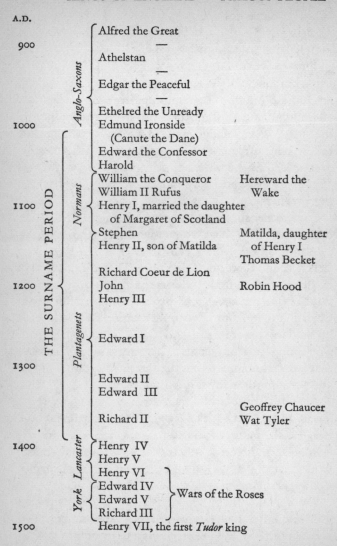

A.D.		KINGS OF ENGLAND	FAMOUS PEOPLE
		Alfred the Great	
900		—	
		Athelstan	
		—	
	Anglo-Saxons	Edgar the Peaceful	
		—	
1000		Ethelred the Unready	
		Edmund Ironside	
		(Canute the Dane)	
		Edward the Confessor	
		Harold	
		William the Conqueror	Hereward the
		William II Rufus	Wake
1100	*Normans*	Henry I, married the daughter	
		of Margaret of Scotland	
		Stephen	Matilda, daughter
		Henry II, son of Matilda	of Henry I
			Thomas Becket
		Richard Coeur de Lion	
1200		John	Robin Hood
		Henry III	
	Plantagenets	Edward I	
1300			
		Edward II	
		Edward III	
			Geoffrey Chaucer
		Richard II	Wat Tyler
1400	*Lancaster*	Henry IV	
		Henry V	
		Henry VI	
	York	Edward IV	Wars of the Roses
		Edward V	
		Richard III	
1500		Henry VII, the first *Tudor* king	

THE SURNAME PERIOD

KINGS OF SCOTLAND WELSH PRINCES

		A.D.
		900
	Howel the Good	
Malcolm I		
—	—	
	Howel the Bad	
	Meredith ab Owain ap	
Malcolm II	Howel	1000
Duncan I	—	
Macbeth	Griffith ap Llewelyn	
Malcolm III, married Margaret,	—	
grand-daughter of Edmund of	Rhys ap Tudor of Powis	
England	—	
Duncan II ⎫	Griffith of Gwynedd	1100
Edgar ⎪		
Alexander I ⎬ their sons		
David I ⎭	Owain ap Griffith	
Malcolm IV		
William the Lion	David ab Owain	
	Llewelyn the Great	1200
Alexander II		
	David ap Llewelyn	
Alexander III	Llewelyn	
	the last Welsh Prince	
Margaret, the maid of Norway	————————	
(War of Independence)		1300
Robert I (*Bruce*), great grandson		
of David I		
David II		
Robert II (*Stewart*), son of Bruce's		
daughter and Walter the Steward		
Robert III		1400
James I		
James II		
James III		
		1500

> *In this Time Chart the dates apply right across both pages showing when these people lived. Short lines indicate that names are omitted but spaces without lines show long reigns.*

nicknames for men, were regular first names for girls before the Norman fashions swept them away. Even as late as 1292 one of the householders who paid a tax for property in London was Sweet Carbonel, probably a widow, for young women with property were quickly married and had nothing of their own as long as their husbands lived. *Carbonell* is a Norman nickname, meaning a little piece of coal, so presumably one of her husband's ancestors was a small dark man, and in all likelihood her children, if she had any, would carry this on. But her first name is English of the old style. A century earlier it was common and must in some cases have provided family names.

It may be that more of our surnames began with women than we can ever recognise for certain.

16 Towns and Villages

It may be seen that a large number of English surnames are formed from Christian names and simply tell that a man was the son of a certain person, but we must still remember the equally great numbers of other kinds. In earlier chapters we spoke of those from occupations and from nicknames, and there is still another source, which is the largest of all – the place where a family lived.

It has already been mentioned that a knight who occupied a manor house and ruled over the village that grew up around it was in most cases known by the village name. Generations passed and still his family belonged there, rebuilding the first rough hall into a small castle or tower of defence, and then enlarging and rebuilding it again to suit a changing world, and all the while he was Robert of Norton or Horton, or whatever the name of the village was. In Norman times when the upper classes spoke French he would be Robert de Norton, and in some families this 'de' has been carefully preserved so that they are still called '*de Havilland*' and so forth. But far more often it was dropped hundreds of years ago. When it was spoken in English the 'of' had always disappeared by 1400 or earlier.

This kind of name was one of the first to stick permanently, and from an early date not only the head of the family and the eldest son who would succeed him but all the family were known by the place-name. And as younger sons often went off to seek their fortunes elsewhere, these village names became scattered throughout England far from their place of origin. Very many of them are to be found in towns from the thirteenth century onwards. In London, for instance, in the reign of Edward I, among the citizens who paid their taxes some can be found whose surnames are village names from every part of England. In most of these cases we can picture a young man setting out from his native village, perhaps riding if he is the son of a knight, perhaps walking with a bundle over his shoulder, travelling day after day towards the wonderful city of which he had heard travellers speak. Such a one was Dick Whittington, a true character, who came from a village of that name where his surname had no doubt been long established, and did in fact become Mayer of London three times over.

There are countless surnames of this type, and hardly a village in England, or town or tiny hamlet that has not provided a name for at least one family. Hundreds of uncommon surnames began in this way, and if you can locate yours as a place in the British Isles – especially if there is only one village of this name – you may be certain that your family lived there in Norman times, though they may have left it almost as long ago. If it is a tiny place, or was so in the Middle Ages, it is quite probable that your ancestors were the principal family there – but the larger the place the less likely this becomes. A big town like *Lincoln* or *Chester* never belonged to just one family. But it would have many young citizens who would go off elsewhere, perhaps alone or perhaps in the service of some lord, and who would be spoken of as coming from this well-known town.

London was always like a magnet drawing young men from all over the country, and few returned from there to settle in country places, as is shown by the fact that *London* itself is a rare surname. All the other county towns, such as *Bedford* and *York*, are more often met with, but they may be somewhat disguised by old forms of spelling, such as *Darby*, *Lester*, *Wooster*, and *Lankester*, while *Bristowe* represents the old pronunciation of Bristol.

Even if you cannot find your surname in a gazetteer there are certain regular endings for names of villages that indicate clearly that they are place names. The commonest English village endings are '-ham' (which is really the same word as 'home') and '-ton' (which is an early form of 'town'). But in the days when the Anglo-Saxons first used this word it only meant a few huts surrounded by a stout palisade. As these settlements grew slowly into large towns, so the meaning of the word grew with them. Another word for a fenced enclosure was 'worth', and any surname ending in this way, such as *Woolworth*, must once have been a village. A more strongly fortified place was called a 'burgh' and this has made the ending of innumerable place names, but it may be spelt 'borough' or 'bury', or even 'berry' which can be misleading. In the North of England a great many places that began as Danish settlements end in '-by', and any name with this ending – such as *Dimbleby* – can only come from a northern village.

One more regular place-name ending is '-ley'. This is the old word 'lea' which meant at first a clearing in the woods and later on a stretch of grass. By itself it has given us the surnames *Lee*, *Leigh* and even *Legge* (for it once had a guttural sound at the end which has long since vanished). People with these names lived 'on the lea'. But it is also an ending for hundreds of village names such as *Bentley*, a village in Lancashire where the lea must have had a lot of coarse 'bent' grass.

Many village names end in '-ingham', '-ington', or '-ingley'. Then we know that each one of these was originally the home or clearing of a tribe or family group, and the first syllable of the word will tell the name of its leader. Thus *Buckingham* was the home of the Buckings, or Buck's people, and *Allington* was the 'tun' or village of Al's family. But such village names are hundreds of years older than our surnames. It was perhaps in the sixth or seventh centuries that Al and Buck built their palisades round their rough huts, and the places were first called by their names, and four or five centuries later that the place-names provided their descendants with permanent surnames even when they went to live elsewhere.

The village names which have been mentioned so far are all typically English, but this kind of surname was also very much used by the Norman knights and barons who followed William the Conqueror to England. Many of them, when they set out on this great adventure, had few possessions but their horses and armour, and were glad to be known by the name of the English manors that were given to them as a reward for their loyalty, and many were known by French nicknames, but the chief of them brought with them the names of the little villages of Normandy where they had lived in wooden castle-keeps. They mostly acquired much greater lands in England and built themselves grander castles, but they were proud of their Norman blood and therefore often preferred to call themselves by the Norman name.

Just as English place names have some very typical endings which help us to recognise many of them, so a few particular French words can help us to pick out Norman places. Any name that includes 'ville' (town), 'court' (an enclosed place) or 'mont' (hill) in any position is sure to be of French origin and is probably Norman. Obvious examples are *Neville*, *Harcourt*, *Beaumont*, and *Montague*, but there are many others that can only be known individually. *Percy* and *Mortimer* for instance began as the names of small villages in Normandy.

All such names originally were spoken with the preposition 'de', but this was generally dropped long ago except when the village name began with a vowel, when it often stuck as part of the name. Thus de Aubigny became *Daubeny*, de Isigny *Disney*, and de Evreux *Devereux*.

Though there are many of these Norman names among us they are a small number compared with the thousands of English origin, and the English village names are just as old and honourable. But long ago all distinction between English and Norman vanished and the two merged together in one nation. Although the Normans were once the rulers of the land, they seem to have vanished away completely, swallowed up in the English people. They married English wives and learnt the English language, and there is little sign of them left, except some of their surnames which they brought with them from their homes in Normandy nine hundred years ago.

Even these have often changed into something that seems very English. *Grenville* has sometimes become *Grenfell*; *Beaumont* exists also as *Beaman*, and *Montford* as *Mumford*, typical examples of Norman knights turned into Englishmen.

17 The Countryside

No surnames are more typical of the English country-side than those that tell where a family lived – not by the name of a special town or village – but by a simple common noun from daily speech, a word like *Hill* or *Meadows* or *Field*.

We see these names in large numbers in the old records where at first they were always part of a complete phrase, Jack on the *Heath*, Hugh by the *Wall*, Richard at the *Lane*. Soon after 1300 the prepositions began to disappear, but occasionally one was left sticking for ever to the noun that followed it, as in the case of *Underwood*. The phrase that stuck most often was 'at the', which was generally written 'atte'. This accounts for such surnames as *Attwell*, *Attwood*, *Attlee* (at the lea), and *Attenborough* (at the borough). It will be seen from the last case that 'atte' sometimes became 'atten', and this happened particularly before a vowel, so that 'atten ash', 'atten oak' and 'atten elms' turned into *Nash* and *Nokes* and *Nelmes*.

We must notice at once that names that sprang from common objects of the countryside had a tendency to acquire an 's' at the end of the word. In the Middle Ages many people lived 'at the Well', later the name was written simply as Well or (Attwell), but later still, for no apparent reason, people began to write *Wells*. Why this happened in some cases and not in others cannot be explained.

This kind of name differs from the proper name of a village in one important way; it always described where a person was living at the time it was spoken. If you call a man Simon of Richmond it was probably in some other place that you used the expression, meaning that he had come from Richmond. But when you spoke of Simon at the *Style* you were thinking of the very spot where his cottage stood. Such a name would be ridiculous twenty miles away where no one could possibly know what stile you had in mind. It was not until a family had been known by one of these simple local words for many generations that it stuck so permanently that it could be used anywhere without anyone's giving a thought to its meaning.

The rule generally holds good that the name of a large place was not given to a man unless he left it. It was useless to call someone *Kent* in Kent, but the smaller the spot described the more likely he was to be living exactly there. If your name was *Oak* or *Noke* you lived right under a splendid oak tree.

There are many tree names among our surnames, *Birch, Beech, Pine*, for instance, and *Rountree* which is the rowan-tree or mountain ash, notable for its scarlet berries. The commonest of them is *Thorne*, the same in meaning as *Hawthorne*, and we must think of the original owner living beside some very ancient gnarled thorn tree which was the most striking feature of his cottage. No one would think of identifying a man's place of residence by such a common sight in the country as a hawthorn unless there was something notable about it. But very old trees were often used as boundary points and landmarks, or sometimes they were the meeting place for the chief men of many villages, a place where the laws had been read out in ancient times. A family known by the simple name of *Tree* must have lived near a specially important one for it to need no further description.

We saw in the last chapter that many families lived 'on the *Lea*', which meant the stretch of grass around which the village had grown up – in fact the village green. The name *Green* often has this same meaning. In the early Subsidy Rolls we can always see clearly when a surname is a local one because then it is written as 'Jacke atte Grene'. When we see 'Jacke en le Grene' (in the green) or just 'Jacke Grene' as we might at the same date, we think of nicknames connected with the May festival (see page 71). It is tiresome when a name has two or more possible meanings like this, but unfortunately it often happens.

Another local name with two meanings is *Moore*. Wild stretches of waste land were called by this word all over the country, and those who lived 'on the moor' were often shepherds or herdsmen. But then again people sometimes called a man a 'Moor' because he had dark colouring (page 89). In early records the meaning is plain, and more often than not it is local.

Many of these local words tell not only where a man lived but what his work was. A 'booth' or 'bothy' was a wooden shed for the cattle, and so also was a 'byre', so anyone called *Booth* or *Byres* probably tended the cattle and slept with them in the straw, while someone called *Faulds* spent his life among the sheep folds. A man who lived by a *Pitt* and took his name from it was very likely engaged in digging something out of it, perhaps gravel or clay or chalk. He might equally be called the *Pitman*; while one who lived in the wood, or close by it, must often have been a woodcutter, or *Woodman*. It is no wonder that *Wood* is one of our commonest local names.

There are many of these pairs of names, *Hill* and *Hillman*, *Poole* and *Pullman*, *Cross* and *Crossman* (he lived at the crossroads). Generally they tell only where the man lived.

England was so full of woods in the Middle Ages that many of them had special names or descriptions. So we have *Broadwood*, *Littlewood*, *Greenwood* as distinct from *Blackwood* of dark pines or yew trees, the *Grisewood* where the pigs were driven ('grice' being an old word for 'swine'), the *Birdwood*, the *Harewood* and many others. Another word meaning 'wood', an old word that has vanished completely from our speech, is *Holt*, while a small wood or clump of trees was a 'grove'. Our many families called *Groves* and *Graves* show how freely this word was once used. *Bygraves* was originally 'by the grove'.

One of the interesting points about our surnames is that they can tell us exactly which words the people of the early Middle Ages used most in their daily talk, and which were hardly known. For instance the land was full of small streams and rivers, and many dwelling places were beside them as everyone needed water, but you will hardly ever meet a family called *Stream*. Instead there are thousands of *Brooks* and *Bournes* (which mean the same thing), and many families lived on their *Banks*. Very small streams were known as *Sykes*.

The word 'valley' had not yet come into the language. Instead a small dip in the land was a *Dean* or a *Dell*. In the North a big valley was a *Dale* and a narrow deep one often called a *Bottom* which has made part of several surnames, like *Winterbottom*, *Ramsbottom* or *Longbottom* which were sheltered hollows in wild, hilly country. In the South-West of England a deep valley was a *Coombe*.

It will be seen that many of these words for local features come from some particular dialect, and though they cannot give the place of origin of a family as closely as the name of a village can, yet they do indicate what part of the country it belongs to. A *Hurst* was a small wood, generally in Kent or Sussex; *Holmes* were low-lying islands, often by a marsh or river in the North-Eastern counties; *Thwaite* and *Royd* are both North country words for clearings in woods. *Briggs* and *Burns* are the Northern or Scottish forms of the Southern *Bridges* and *Bourne*.

The study of place names is a large and complicated subject, and these few examples must serve to show how many surnames come from local words, some of them still in use, others little known today. Many are made up of two words that describe a particular spot vividly for us, if only we will stop to think about it. *Ashcroft* meant a small enclosed field among ash trees,

Thorndyke a ditch lined with hawthorns, *Whitaker* a ploughed field (acre) with white chalky soil, *Townsend* the last house at the very end of the town or village.

Some describe the actual house where our ancestors once lived – *Moorhouse*, a house on the moor; *Woodhouse*, in or near the wood; *Brighouse*, by the bridge or perhaps even on it; *Hobhouse*, the house where Hob (or Robin) lives; *Lofthouse* (sometimes shortened to *Loftus*), a house with a loft or upper storey. There are plenty more of this sort and anyone can find amusement in making such collections.

18 Nationalities

In the early Middle Ages it was quite usual to describe a foreigner simply as *Strange*, but if you knew where he had come from you might say more precisely that he was *French*, or *Dench* which was one way of saying Danish. (The more ordinary form of this word was 'Denish' which has become confused with the Christian name *Dennis*.) But by the time surnames were becoming general the Danes who had settled in England were so well mixed with the English that they were hardly foreigners at all.

It sounds contradictory to say that a surname like *French* is truly English, but it was only in England that it could be given, and only at a very early date, or the man in question would have had a surname of his own. We have seen in other chapters that most of the leading Norman families brought their French surnames to

England with them, but many of their followers had none, and some of them were simply described as *Norman* or *French* (from the language they spoke) by the English people among whom they settled.

In reverse *Langlais*, which means 'Englishman', is a regular old surname in France.

These racial names are worth a little thought because they show us something of the different foreign strains that came to swell the population of England during the surname period. In modern times, particularly in the last hundred years, people have come from all the countries of the world, and in all our big cities we have a sprinkling of surnames that are obviously of foreign origin. But this is another matter, which we will think of in Chapter 20. We are now concerned with names that grew in this island out of our own speech and thought, the names that really belong to the English-speaking world.

One of the racial names that is oldest established in England is *Fleming*. William the Conqueror's wife, Matilda, was the daughter of the Count of Flanders and a number of her countrymen came with her to England. Later on, on several occasions, groups of Flemings were invited to England and persuaded to settle in places where they would be useful. They were clever, hardworking people, good at various crafts and particularly skilful at weaving. As their own small country was often over-crowded they were glad to be given homes in England and played an important part in developing the cloth trade. English craftsmen did not always like them, perhaps because they were so industrious, but they prospered and their descendants are with us still.

Then there were the Bretons, who from ancient times had been closely in touch with Cornwall across the sea. Here again we can see the influence of William the Conqueror's friends and relations. One of his kinsmen was Count Alan of Brittany, who brought a large company of Bretons to fight at Hastings, and afterwards married one of William's daughters. He was given extensive lands in Lincolnshire and Yorkshire which he divided out among his many followers. *Bretton*, *Britten*, *Britain* and *Brett* are all derived from their nationality, and of course the name Alan became popular, especially in the North-eastern counties, resulting in the frequent surname *Allen*.

Other racial names from Europe include *Gascoigne*, *Gaskin*, or *Gaskain*, all coming from Gascony and probably all originally concerned with the importation of wine from that sunny land which was one of the possessions of the kings of England in the twelfth century. Then there is *Burgoyne* from Burgundy, *Pettingell* from Portugal, and *Romer* from Rome. Most of the people who were given such names in England and whose families settled here must have been merchants or seamen. The English did not always pronounce these foreign places very accurately. Genoa sometimes became *Jannaway* and Venice *Venus*.

Some other names which seem to be of the same sort are misleading. *Holland*, for instance, may come from an English village of this name – there are three of them; it just means 'high land' as also does the name of the country we call Holland. The Dutch use it for only a part of their land which is a little higher than the rest. *German* is very often from the Christian name Germain which was quite popular among the Normans because of an early Bishop of Gaul, St Germain. On the other hand *Francis*, which sounds more like a Christian name, nearly always meant simply 'French'. We can see it frequently in early records as 'le franceys', the Frenchman.*

But when we think of the people of other races who made their permanent homes among the English so long ago that their nationality provided them with surnames, by far the largest groups are those of the Celtic countries that border England, particularly Wales and Scotland.

Welsh is an English word which originally meant 'a foreigner' and was applied to the people of the West who spoke an unknown tongue. Before the Conquest it was 'wealh'; soon after it appears as Walysh or Walys, and although in the standard language it has settled down as Welsh, the surnames it has produced include *Wallis*, *Wallace*, *Walsh* and *Welch*. The first two forms are the oldest and can only have come into England or Scotland so long ago that the link with Wales is remote indeed.

The name *Scott* can be found in all parts of England, even the South, from the eleventh century onwards, proving that Scots have always been inclined to travel, as they still are, and brought with them a distinctive character known and recognised everywhere. This name is common in its own country too, partly because in early times its people were made up of several races, and the Scots (who had confusingly come originally from Ireland) were distinct from the others until gradu-

* It was only after the death of Francis of Assisi that it became widespread as a first name, too late to have much effect on our surnames.

ally their name spread over the whole country. We must also remember that among the wild hills of the Border-country there were constant raids and skirmishes between *Scott* and *English*. National pride was strong, and these words must have been often on men's lips.

Next we must think of the Cornish, who, although their land was part of England in the surname period, yet spoke a language of their own which made them seem like foreigners. They had some very distinctive surnames of their own, nearly all being the names of their Cornish homes, and many of them beginning with 'Tre' (which means a homestead). There is no mistaking where names like *Trevelyan* and *Trethowan* come from. But if we think, not of their own surnames, but of those that were given them by the English when they first settled among them, we shall find *Cornish* and its older form *Cornwallis*, as well as good numbers of *Cornwall*, *Cornwell* and *Cornell*.

Compared with these other racial names *Irish* and *Ireland* are very uncommon, showing that, in the days when such surnames were given verbally to new-comers, few Irishmen found their way to England. But they have amply made up for this in recent years complete with surnames of their own.

In fact wherever English-speaking people are gathered all over the world today, Irish, Scottish and Welsh names that had developed in their own countries will be found among them. So much so that we must give these three Celtic countries a chapter to themselves.

19 Wales, Scotland and Ireland

The Welsh were very late in establishing fixed surnames. Any of them who settled in England at an early date would soon be given a second name in the English fashion, but in their own country until about 1500 one name was enough for ordinary use, with perhaps a nickname to help it. When they wanted to specify someone more exactly they would recite a whole list of his ancestors – 'Hugh-ap-Morgan-ap-David-ap-Howel' and so on. 'Ap' means 'son of'.

When Henry VII, who was himself the son of a Welshman, came to the throne of England in 1485, he urged his countrymen to adopt permanent surnames like the English, and from that time they began gradually to do so, each family keeping to the name of one ancestor instead of changing with each generation. But this sytem unfortunately led to a decided lack of variety, for except for a very few old-established nicknames, such as *Lloyd* (grey), *Gough* (red), *Wynn* or *Gwynn* (white), and *Vaughan* (little), all Welsh surnames are formed from men's Christian names and some are shared by too many families. Among themselves the Welsh often make up for this deficiency by speaking of 'Mrs Jones, Chapel', or 'Jones, the Milk', but these extra items of information have never made official surnames in Wales as they did so freely at an earlier date in England. Another answer to the problem is the double surname.

As Welsh has always been an entirely separate language from English it has its own distinctive personal names, many of great antiquity. *Morgan*, *Meredith*, *Griffith*, *Owen*, *Howell* and *Llewellyn* are all the names of famous princes from early times (see page 105) given here in modern English spelling. Another of the same sort is *Rhys* which the English have turned into *Rees*, *Reece* and *Rice*.

Such names may easily be recognised as Welsh in origin, but it happened that during the Middle Ages the Norman and Biblical names which had become so popular in England spread also into Wales, and just at the time that surnames were being fixed there in the largest numbers the English favourites John, William, Robert, Hugh and a few more were so popular that they have provided more family names for the Welsh than their own native names have done. At first they were written 'ap-William' and so on, but soon the 'ap' was dropped, and instead a final 's' or 'es' was added in the English style, making such names as *Williams*. *Roberts* and *Hughes*. These names could also be English in origin, but it is the Welsh who are responsible for

125

their large numbers, especially in the case of *Jones* which echoes their pronunciation of John.

But although the addition of 's' to the full Christian name became the regular way of making surnames in Wales, the native 'ap' has left a more permanent mark than you might think. When the Christian name began with an R or an H the -p often stuck to it, making *Pritchard* or *Pritchett* from ap-Richard, *Price* from ap-Rhys, *Pugh* from ap-Hugh, *Parry* or *Perry* from ap-Harry, *Powell* from ap-Howell, and others like *Probert* and *Prodger* that are easy to identify. Before a vowel 'ap' becomes 'ab' and so ab-Owen often produced *Bowen*, while the popular Welsh name Evan gives *Bevan* as well as *Evans*.

The surname *Lewis* comes occasionally from the French Louis but it is far more often from Llewi, short for the famous name of Llewellyn the Great, and of his grandson, the last independent Prince of Wales. It was in 1284 that Edward I conquered this country, united it with England and gave the title to his baby son. Ever since then the Welsh have spread freely into England, and their names are mingled with the English everywhere.

In contrast to those of Wales the surnames of Scotland are very varied. They belong to two distinct groups the Lowlands and the Highlands, where the way of life and the language itself was different.

The Lowlands of Scotland had once been part of the Old English kingdom of Northumbria, and the people spoke, as they still do, a northern form of English. They adopted surnames a little later than in England, but when they did they were of the same four types. There are differences of dialect, of course; *Long* and *Strong* in

England are *Lang* and *Strang* in Scotland; *Church* in England is *Kirk* in Scotland, and some other examples of northern pronunciation are given on page 117, but in general the names are very similar. Old Scottish personal names like *Duncan* and *Malcolm* are well represented, but newer fashions also spread from England, making *Wilson* and *Johnson* as common in Edinburgh as in London. Naturally the names of Scotland's own kings became popular. Some of the early ones were Alexander, David and Robert, which in due course produced their own crop of *Sandersons*, *Davidsons* and *Robertsons*.*

The Normans did not conquer Scotland, but many of them settled there peacefully and founded important families. Both *Bruce* and *Baliol*, names famous in Scottish history, come from villages in Normandy. The names of many Scottish villages, such as *Crawford* and *Moffatt*, are well-known surnames too; while names from occupations were much the same as south of the border.

But in the Highlands the whole system of naming was different. In those bare, wild hills life was hard and men could only live and bring up their families in safety by being banded together in great clans, sharing their scanty food and standing together in every danger. The surname was the clan name, and loyalty to its leader was so important that the name was cherished proudly even though it was not very useful for distinguishing one person from another. Within the clan, nicknames were much in use; Rob Roy, for instance, was a *MacGregor*, but Roy (the red) served as a second name among his own people.

*See page 105.

The Highlanders spoke Gaelic, and most of their clan names belong to that language, being the personal names of famous chieftains, with the addition of 'Mac'. This well-known beginning means 'son of – ' or 'descendant of – ', but was freely used by all loyal followers, so that names like *MacDonald*, *Mackenzie* and *Macmillan* were multiplied by thousands as their clans grew. Sometimes the original tribal leader was remembered by a nickname, such as *Cameron*, which meant 'crooked nose', and *Campbell*, 'crooked mouth', and these too were adopted by members of the clan. But not all clan names are Gaelic. *Grant*, for instance, is of French origin (see page 52) and *Stewart* (page 44) comes from an English word.

Though Scots from the Lowlands came into England from early times, there is little sign of Highlanders in English records before the eighteenth century. Since then they have had many troubles in their own country, and have overflowed from their wild hills, scattering the whole English-speaking world with Macs.

The chief distinction of Irish names is that they are so old, probably the oldest surnames in Europe. In the Dark Ages when much of Europe was still heathen, Ireland was known as a land of saints and scholars, and in some respects was more advanced in civilisation than any of its neighbours. The heathen Vikings who troubled so many places in the tenth century put an end to Ireland's golden age, but already many of its people had regular surnames which have continued all through its history and are still prominent today. These old Irish surnames nearly all come from the names of ancestors or tribal leaders from that early time. The typical beginning, 'O'', as in *O'Neill*, *O'Connor*,

O'Connell, *O'Brien* and many more, has much the same meaning as Mac. Niall, Conor, Conal and Brian are four of the heroic kings from Ireland's early history. The O' is often dropped from these surnames in England.

Mac was also used in the same way as in Scotland; and the Irish Macs, which include many well-known surnames, such as *MacCarthy*, have so many different forms and spellings that they seem endless. In the London Telephone Directory over six hundred different names begin with Mac or Mc, and more than half of them are Irish.

The commonest Irish surname is *Murphy*, of which the original meaning was 'sea wanderer'. Another well-known one is *Kennedy*, which means 'ugly head', and like the Gaelic Cameron and Campbell must have begun with an affectionate joke about a leader who was not a beauty. The Kennedy who first made this name honoured was the father of the great Brian Boru, King of all Ireland, who defeated the invading Danes in battle in 1014. A nickname with a better meaning is *Sullivan*, 'black-eyed'.

Although many Irish names date from before the Conquest of England, the Normans, who influenced so many countries, had their effect on Ireland too. In the reign of Henry II an army from England was sent to conquer it for the English king. The Norman barons who led this enterprise were more or less successful but they mostly settled in Ireland and never came back, and their surnames have continued there ever since. One famous family who established themselves in Ireland at this time were the *Fitzgeralds*. Fitz was a corrupted short form of the Latin *filius* meaning 'son'. It was used by the Normans in England (though never in France), and though a few families have kept it ever since then (*Fitzwilliam*, *Fitzsimmons* and others) it was generally dropped long ago. But in Ireland the three sons of Gerald of Windsor, who all took the surname Fitzgerald in the twelfth century, have countless descendants who have kept it in full. And even the name of Ireland's patron saint is common in the Norman form of *Fitzpatrick*.

We might sum up these mainly Celtic lands by saying that the Welsh, Highland and Irish surnames are nearly all patronymic, coming from the personal names of ancestors or chieftains. The Irish and Highland names are both much older than the Welsh and have more variety. Lowland names are almost indistinguishable from those in the North of England. All of these have mingled with the English, especially in modern times, and are now to be found with them all over the world.

20 Names from Many Lands

In Chapter 18 we thought of some of the surnames that the English gave to foreigners who settled among them in the Middle Ages, names that have long been entirely English. We must now take a brief glance at some of the thousands of families who have made their homes in Britain in modern times, bringing their own foreign surnames and adding even more variety to what was already a rich mixture.

French names have come in at all periods since the Norman Conquest. The earlier ones, as we have seen, were thoroughly adopted and made English, but more recent arrivals have generally kept their French character. There were, for instance, thousands of Protestants – known as Huguenots – expelled from France because of their religion in 1685, and many of them settled here. And we must not forget our own Channel Islanders, who are not foreign at all but have French names inherited from the time when they all spoke French. Their surnames keep the French spelling but are often pronounced in English style. A typical one is *Le Mesurier*, the measurer. In Franch many surnames keep the definite article as this one does – *Leclerc*, the clerk, *Lenoir*, the black. In England it was dropped very early.

In the nineteenth century many people from all parts of Europe settled in England because it was so prosperous, a land of opportunity. Now it is no longer rich, but still better off than some places, and it has the great advantage that all comers can practise their own religions and express their opinions freely. So immigrants still come, and in larger numbers than ever.

We think first of the Jews, a race that has been persecuted for centuries throughout Europe. In 1290 Edward I expelled them all from England and it was not till 1654 that the ban against them was lifted. Even then it was a long time before many came to settle here again, but in the last hundred years they have come in large numbers, especially when they suffered the worst treatment of all under the rule of the Nazis.

Jewish surnames have not been hereditary very long and few go back in the same family much before 1800. The commonest among them is *Cohen*, which means a priest, and another of the same sort is *Levi*, often written *Levy* or *Levin* and in other ways too. The Levites acted as assistants to the priests in the synagogues. Apart from these priestly names the Jews used patronymics, each man naming his father, and as they were always faithful to the memory of their great leaders of Old Testament times, this resulted in very many Jewish surnames derived from Abraham, Isaac, Jacob, Moses, Solomon and so on. A few of these (with the usual addition of 's' may have an English origin, see page 83) but the majority are Jewish.

But because the Jews have been dispersed so long among many lands their surnames are considerably varied; for in spite of their loyalty to their own religion they have adapted themselves in many ways to the countries where they have lived, modifying their names to the different languages. Thus the family who would become *Abrahams* in England would be *Abramski* in Poland or *Brahms* in Germany. They were also inclined to adopt the local names.

In the late eighteenth century several of the German states passed laws compelling Jews to take permanent surnames by which they could be recognised. They were not to be any names used by other people, but newly made up out of words with plain meanings. Naturally the Jews chose pleasant subjects, such as *Rosenbaum* (rose tree) and *Blumenfeld* (flower field), and many families now in England have these names, though often shortened and spelt in the English way, as, for example, *Bloom*.

In this century the Jews have come to England mostly from Germany and Poland. Many non-Jewish people have also come from these countries; for example, from Poland thousands came to join in the war against Nazi Germany and then chose to stay here. Their names are very distinctive, with the typical endings -ewicz (son of) and -ski (belonging to). Polish names look difficult to us because their spelling habits are different. Their 'sz' is like our 'sh'; 'cz' like our 'ch'; and 'rz' is the sound in the middle of 'measure'. W is like V or F. They are inclined to put a lot of consonants together, but who are we to complain of such things? Many foreigners think our spelling is dreadful, and find some of our sounds, such as 'th', extremely hard to say.

The European countries where surnames were first firmly established for most of the people are Italy, France and England, with the German-speaking lands just a little later. Last of all come the Scandinavians (page 12). Old surnames, formed from informal talk in the days when few could write, are always immensely varied compared with those deliberately taken much later, and the same lively mixture that we have in England exists also across the Channel. French surnames are similar in style to ours; they have the same regular types and the same profusion of affectionate diminutive forms that can turn one name into half a dozen more. The Italians also have endless diminutives. Their commonest surname is *Rossi* (red), not that they had so many redheads among them but those they had were noticed (just as *Schwartz*, meaning black, is common among the fair-haired Germans). Rossi has branched into *Rossini*, *Rossetti*, *Rosselli* and several more.

Right across Europe the same surnames can be found in the different languages. The smith, so important in medieval life, has left his trail everywhere: *Herrara* in Spain, *Ferrari* in Italy, *Lefevre* in France, *Schmitt* in Germany, *Smidt* in Holland, *Kovacs* in Hungary, *Kowalski* in Poland; while the nickname *Brown* is paralleled even more closely, from *Lebrun* and *Brunel* in France to *Bronowski* in Poland; and the names of the Christian saints are echoed in endless variety.

All these countries have links of culture and tradition; but in the last hundred years newcomers have flocked into Britain from much father afield than Europe and from totally different backgrounds of language and custom. It is useless to expect their names to fit into our patterns.

The Chinese, for instance, have hereditary surnames that are far older than any in Europe. They are more like clan names, for there are only about 440 of them (they are exactly listed) to over 700 million people. They are placed first with the other more personal names following, and these are much more varied. The surnames are very short and many have nature themes -*Li* is a plum tree, *Lee* a pear tree – but because of their great age their meanings are often obscure.

But the most notable influx of foreign names in modern times has come from India and Pakistan. It was only in 1947 that these two became separate countries and later still that East Pakistan became Bangladesh, but they all contain something of the same complicated mixture of races, religions and languages.

Nearly all Pakistanis are Moslems – followers of Mohammed – and the names they use are found among Moslems everywhere. For when a man was converted to this faith he always took completely new names, expressing his belief in it. These might include the name of its founder, *Mohammed*, or that of his faithful son-in-law, *Ali*. Moslem names are mostly words for virtues or high ideals. Ali means 'high', *Ahmed* 'praise', *Hussain* 'excellence', *Din* 'faith', *Rahman* 'merciful', *Aziz* 'dear'. Among themselves Moslems do not use surnames as we do, but they have a number of titles of honour such as *Khan* and *Shah* which might signify great rulers, but are often added to men's names as no more than vague terms of respect, rather like the English 'Esquire'. Others of this sort are *Malik* (king) and *Mirza* (prince). When a Pakistani or Indian Moslem feels in need of a surname because of contact with the West, it is often one of this kind that he adopts.

The great majority of Indians are Hindus and on their names, too, the influence of religion is very great. Many personal names echo those of gods and legendary heroes such as Rama, the warrior, and Krishna, the charioteer, both re-incarnations of the god Vishnu. *Ram* and *Krishna* are often used as personal names, either alone or with a lot more added, for Hindu names are apt to be very long – especially in southern India – but such names would not normally pass from father to son.

In India there is no regular system of surnames as we have, though with the spread of Western customs there is now a strong movement in that direction. However, among some groups the same names have long been used by the same families, expecially among the higher castes. The Brahmans (or priests) for instance are divided into many castes each with its own name, of which *Chatterji* and *Mukherji* are typical in Bengal. The -ji at the end (often spelt -gee) is a term of respect rather like 'the reverend'.

Most Asian names are rendered into English in a great variety of spellings. Another that comes in many forms is *Chaudhuri*, which signifies a village headman in Bengal or the Punjab. The same name is expressed in another language by the name *Patel*, in the western part of India near Bombay. Thousands of Indians from that region migrated first to Uganda but have now found new homes here.

Another important religion from the Indian subcontinent is that of the Sikhs who have a language and customs of their own, and may be easily recognised by their turbans. In the seventeenth century when they were threatened by enemies their leader adopted the title of *Singh*, meaning lion, as a symbol of the courage they must show. Since then every Sikh includes Singh among his names, and many of them use it as a surname in England. But it is not only a Sikh name. Some Indians who are not Sikhs use it too.

There is no room here to speak of immigrants from other lands who have brought unfamiliar names into Britain; but one large group must be mentioned – the West Indians – whose names, in contrast to those of the Asians, are indistinguishable from our own. Of course their origin has nothing whatever to do with India – that was Columbus's big mistake. Far in the past their roots are African, but there is nothing African about their names. In the long time of their slavery those who lived in islands owned by Britain spoke English as their natural language and used English-type names, and when they were all made free those who had one name only and needed another adopted any that they heard around them. Many took the names of the owners of the plantations where they had worked, or of someone they liked and admired. So their names may be English, Welsh or Scottish, though not inherited in the same way as if their ancestors had lived in Britain. There is a mixture among them too. Their islands were once part of the Spanish Main and some have Spanish names; and after slavery was abolished a good many Asians were brought in to work in the plantations, so East Indian names are not uncommon. West Indians here must miss their hot sun and blue sea, but at least in the way of language and names they should feel at home.

One way and another, surnames in England have become a great mixture, but this is chiefly in the big cities where the newcomers go to find work. Indeed there are plenty of small country towns where you will hardly see a foreign name. And to balance the mixture here we must remember that British surnames have gone out over the world in far greater numbers than others have come in. In North America, Australia, New Zealand and other lands overseas there are millions of families whose surnames arose in this island before the New World was even discovered.

21 Problems to Solve

The study of surnames is like a gigantic puzzle that can never be finished. It presents endless problems, some very easy, some needing investigation, many so hard that we can never be sure we have found the right answer. Even leaving aside the foreign names mixed in with ours and concentrating on those that belong to our own language, we will never understand them all. Some surnames have several possible origins; others have baffled the most learned scholars. Even a name which has an obvious origin, proved by examples from medieval records, may still in some special case have arisen in a different way.

In spite of all these difficulties, hundreds of surnames can be clearly explained and understood. In this book we have concentrated mostly on those that exist in large numbers, because once you have grasped the normal regular ways in which such names developed, you will find it much easier to see how more unusual ones fit into the pattern.

The great thing is to think about family names as real words with meanings, and in many cases the sense will stand out before you the minute you look for it. You may have known a Mr *Newman* for years and spoken the name a hundred times without ever stopping to think of the 'new man' who once came to settle in a place where he was a stranger and newcomers were rare. Nothing could be easier. *Newcombe* is just a little harder because the spelling is deceptive, but it is only 'new come'. Many names that consist of ordinary words still in use go unrecognised simply because of their spelling.

It was not until the eighteenth century that the spelling of English became fixed in a standard form, but this had nothing to do with surnames, and every family has always been free to follow its own fancy in this respect. In the sixteenth and seventeenth centuries the same man might write his surname in a dozen or more different ways, and by the time it became usual to settle on one spelling and stick to it, most people had forgotten the origins of their names, or even wished to disguise them, or gave no thought to the matter at all. So spelling is often more of a hindrance than a help in trying to find a true origin.

Surnames, then, are problems to be solved. There is always an answer, but it may be hard to find, and harder still to be sure of.

Let us suppose that you do not know the meaning of your surname and cannot find it in this book, or any other that you have available on the subject. This is quite likely, for there are more different surnames than anyone has ever been able to count, and no writer has ever tried to deal with them all. Besides, you want to find out for yourself if possible. The first thing to do is to see if the name can be divided into separate parts which may show what type it belongs to. If it has a local ending such as '-brook' or 'field', or'-ham' or '-by' or one of the others mentioned in Chapters 16 and 17, or others still that you can discover for yourselves, then you can at least be sure that it is the name of a place. The next step is to look in a gazetteer to see if you can find it. In any case it is always worth while trying a gazetteer, as more rare surnames come from place-names than from any other source, and many small villages that you may never have heard of have very odd names that do not sound like places at all.

If this fails, try a dictionary, but it must be a big one that gives some etymology or history of words. The *Shorter Oxford Dictionary* (which is not very short, being two big volumes) includes hundreds of rare and obsolete words which few people know, although they may have been common once. Supposing your name ends in '-er'; this suggests an occupation – though it is not always so – and there are many specialised or old-fashioned tasks that are now unfamiliar. For instance, you probably have no idea what a *Tedder* would do, but you can find out from the dictionary, if you take a little trouble. It comes under 'ted' which means 'to spread out or rake, especially in the case of new-mown grass'. You can see now that a 'tedder' was a useful man in a village, probably one who was always called in to help with the hay making.

Again, you might wonder what the surname *Crowder*

could mean. Someone who gets into crowds does not seem to make much sense. The dictionary will tell you that a 'crowd', besides meaning a lot of people, was a name for a kind of fiddle played in the Middle Ages, and a 'crowder' the man who played it. *Fiddler* became a surname too, but 'crowder' (or *Crowther* as it was sometimes written) was then the more usual word.

If you find a word in a dictionary which seems to fit the surname you are studying, be sure that it is old enough. Remember that except for some of the surnames from Christian names that were established late in Wales or Scotland, practically all our surnames were formed before 1400, and any name that appears to come from a more modern word must be suspect. For instance, you might think that the surname *Muskett* came from an early kind of gun. But the *Oxford Dictionary* will tell you that this meaning of the word is not recorded before 1579. It also gives the earlier meaning of the same word which was 'the male of the sparrowhawk'. So we discover that this surname is one of the many bird nicknames, associated with falconry. Incidentally, we see too, how this kind of gun when newly invented took its name from a bird that could kill in the sky.

The English language as it was spoken before 1066 is called Old English, from that date to 1500 it is Middle English. Any word which is given as belonging to O.E. or M.E. in the dictionary may have formed a surname, but if it is not classed as either of these it is too late, and another origin must be looked for.

Any surname that includes 'kin' or 'kins' must be from a Christian name, so also must one that ends in '-cock' unless it is from a real bird like a *Woodcock*.

Sometimes the pet-name that makes the first syllable is so brief that one can hardly tell what it comes from. *Makinson*, for instance, is from *Matthew*. *Hankin* and *Hancock* show that Han was a popular short form of some Christian name. But which? It is probably a very early form of John, from Johan.

A surname ending in '-ing' is almost always from an Old English personal name or nickname. The only exceptions are a few place-names, but they too originated from the names of people or tribes. These '-ing' names are among the oldest and most typically English of all our surnames.

These are just a few of the ways in which you can set about trying to find meanings of surnames, or at least see what type of name they belong to. You can never be quite sure that you have found the right origin of a difficult surname unless you have seen it in its earliest stages in medieval records, and few people have the opportunity to do that sort of work. But at least you can take an interest in names, identify a great many, and enjoy trying to solve the problems presented by others.

When you have thought about your own surname you can go on to the others in your family. Your grandparents provide you with four which all belong to you in a way, and perhaps the older members of your family can tell you of others further back. Family history can be fascinating.

But there is no need to stop at your own family. Look at the surnames all around you and see what you can make of them. Some may be foreign and you can try to guess where they came from, but most of them are part of our own language – a part that became

fossilised long ago. But though like fossils they preserve old forms, they are still very much alive. They
are probably our oldest personal possessions, but none
the worse for their age, and still in constant use.

And the study of surnames has one great advantage
over collecting fossils, in that material for it is so
abundant and can be found almost anywhere. You can
never be bored, even waiting for a bus, once you have
discovered that the names all about you are full of
human history for you to discover if only you will look
at them and think.

Sources and Further Reading

The medieval names used as examples in this book are taken mostly from:

The Anglo-Saxon Chronicle.
Domesday Book.
The Lay Subsidy Rolls of Edward I, II and III.
The Poll Tax of Richard II.

Fuller details of these and other original sources used in this book are given in *English Surnames* by the same author (see below).

Books recommended for further information about surnames and their origins:

A Dictionary of British Surnames, P. H. Reaney, London, 1958.
The Origins of British Surnames, P. H. Reaney, London, 1967.
Surnames of Scotland, G. F. Black, New York, 1946.
The Surnames of Ireland, E. MacLysaght, Irish Universities Press, 1969.
How you got your name, J. Pennethorne Hughes, London, 1959.
English Surnames, C. M. Matthews, London, 1966.

Reference books that should be useful in searching for meanings yourself:

The Shorter Oxford English Dictionary.
The Concise Dictionary of Middle English, Skeat, Oxford.

The Oxford Dictionary of English Christian Names,
    E. G. Withycombe.

The Oxford Dictionary of English Place-Names,
    E. Ekwall.

Gazetteer of the British Isles, Bartholomew.

Index of Surnames

Abbot(t), 40–1
Abraham(s), 83, 133
Abramski, 133
Adams, 83
Adamson, 83
Adcock, 65
Addis, 83
Addison, 83
Adkins, 83
Ahmed, 135
Albert, 97
Alden, 97
Aldridge, 97
Alfred, 95–6
Algar, 97
Ali, 135
Allbright, 97
Allen, 121
Allington, 110
Allison, 100
Alston, 97
Ambler, 54
Anderson, 83
Andrews, 83
Angel, 69
Anthony, 91
Archer, 45, 47
Armour, 24
Armstrong, 13
Arrow, 54
Arrowsmith, 24
Ashcroft, 117
Atherston, 97

Atkins, 83
Atkinson, 83
Attenborough, 113
Attlee, 113
Attwell, 113
Attwood, 113
Auden, 97
Austin, 91
Aylmer, 97
Aylwin, 97
Aziz, 133

Bailey, 32
Baines, 53
Baker, 7, 16, 21
Baliol, 127
Ballard, 52
Banks, 117
Barber, 11
Barker, 18
Baron, 72
Bartelmy, 83
Bartholomew, 83
Bartlett, 83
Bassett, 53
Batchelor, 9
Bates, 83
Batten, 83
Baxter, 21
Bayliss, 32
Beaman, 112
Beaton, 103
Beatty, 103

More Beaver Books

We hope you have enjoyed this Beaver Book. Here are some of the other titles:

Battles and Battlefields David Scott Daniell brings to life fifteen of the most important battles fought in Britain between 1066 and 1746; with strategic maps and other illustrations by William Stobbs

The Tower and the Traitors The amazing stories of just some of the men and women who have lived and died in the Tower of London; told by Barbara Leonie Picard

A Knight and his Castle What it was like to live in a castle; by R. Ewart Oakeshott

Through the Fire The exciting story of how two Quaker children rescue their father from Bridewell gaol during the Great Fire of London in 1666; by Hester Burton

The Crocodile Based on the true story of Mary Anning, John Tully's novel for older children is set in Lyme Regis and tells of Mary's search for fossils – especially the famous 'Crocodile' – against a background of the Napoleonic Wars. With illustrations by Clifford Bayly

My Favourite Escape Stories Pat Reid, author of *The Colditz Story*, presents his favourite true stories from four hundred years of escapes. Gripping reading for everyone from nine upwards

New Beavers are published every month and if you would like the *Beaver Bulletin* – which give all the details – please send a large stamped addressed envelope to:

Beaver Bulletin
The Hamlyn Group
Astronaut House
Feltham
Middlesex TW14 9AR